An Hachette UK company
www.hachette.co.uk

First published in Great Britain in 2012 by Godsfield Press,
a division of Octopus Publishing Group Ltd,
Endeavour House, 189 Shaftesbury Avenue, London WC2H 8JY
www.octopusbooks.co.uk
www.octopusbooksusa.com

Distributed in the US by Hachette Book Group USA,
237 Park Avenue, New York NY 10017 USA

Distributed in Canada by Canadian Manda Group,
165 Dufferin Street, Toronto, Ontario, Canada M6K 3H6

ISBN: 978-1-84181-355-4

A CIP catalogue record of this book is available from the British Library.

Printed and bound in China.

1 3 5 7 9 10 8 6 4 2

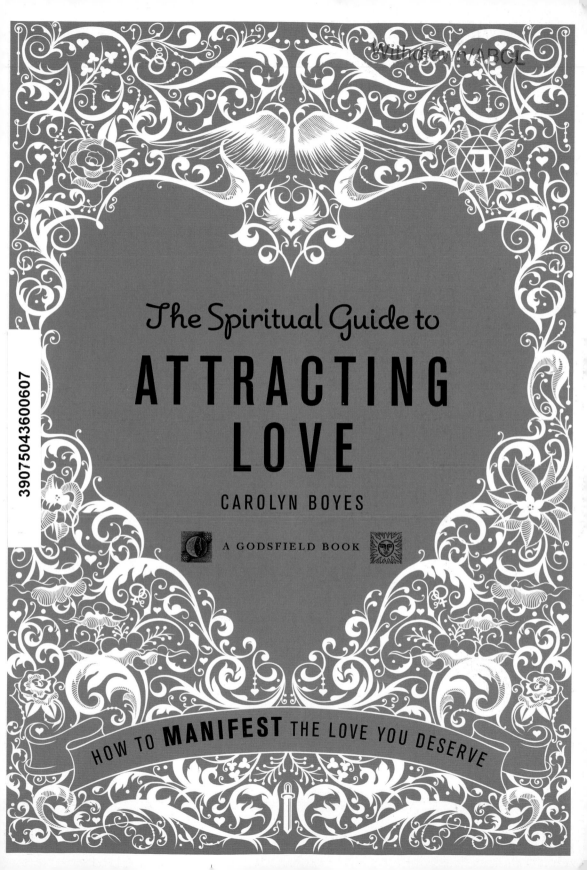

The Spiritual Guide to

ATTRACTING LOVE

CAROLYN BOYES

A GODSFIELD BOOK

HOW TO **MANIFEST** THE LOVE YOU DESERVE

Contents

Introduction

'GREAT THINGS ARE NOT DONE BY IMPULSE,
BUT BY A SERIES OF SMALL THINGS
BROUGHT TOGETHER.'
VINCENT VAN GOGH

Have you ever wondered what it will take to find someone who really loves you?

Is it your greatest wish to be loved by someone who loves you as much as you love them?

Is it your dream to live a life where you can be yourself, perhaps surrounded by loving friends, partner and family?

Maybe more than anything you just yearn to love yourself and to be comfortable with your own company.

This book will show you how to use the Law of Attraction and the wisdom of some of the most ancient spiritual traditions on the planet in order to attract love into your life, helping you to heal past wounds and to live a nurturing joyful life. Using simple but effective techniques and rituals, you will learn to empower yourself to manifest the changes you want in your life. You don't need to believe in a particular religion or faith – the ways of thinking and techniques are suitable whatever your background or culture. Even if you have already looked into manifestation, visualization, goal-setting or cosmic ordering, if you haven't yet got what you want, I believe this book can help.

What is love?

Love has been baffling humans for thousands of years. What is it? It has been described in the past as a power with more force than a besieging army or a priceless commodity because it is the only thing you can give away and still keep. What does love mean for you?

We all have our own definitions of love. However, I think it is universally accepted that love is a basic human need. From the moment we leave the womb to the moment of death, we all share this need to feel love.

This book is focused primarily on romantic relationships, showing you how to attract a loving partner into your life. At the same time, love can come to us in many forms throughout our lives: in the form of loving platonic friendships, family love, the love of children, and of course love from a romantic partner.

The love-attraction formula

This book introduces ways in which you can bring love into your life. These fit into a basic method, which I call the Love-attraction Formula. When you follow this formula you can change your life and bring into it the love you desire in whatever form you want it.

Step 1: Believe

Examine and, if necessary, change your beliefs. According to the Law of Attraction, we manifest what we believe we can attract. The Law of Attraction is powered by thought. Even if we are not consciously aware of this fact, our thoughts make sure that we bring into existence the sort of life we believe both that we can have and that we deserve to have. In Chapters 1 and 2 we take a look at how this works in practice and you will encounter some case studies about people who have changed their lives by learning to change their beliefs. Sometimes changing your thoughts is a very simple process – recognizing what they are, identifying new beliefs and adopting them. Sometimes, if we have had particularly damaging life experiences, some healing of the past is required first.

Step 2: Become loving

Treat yourself in exactly the way you wish others to treat you. In Chapter 3 I explain how 'love equals love'. When you love yourself and don't need other people to make you happy, you will paradoxically attract more people who want to make you happy and love you.

Step 3: Decide your future

Identify what you really want to manifest in your life. Our intentions as well as our beliefs are the key to what we attract in life. If you have a vision that is possible, if not probable, to achieve, then as long as your beliefs support you, you will be able to achieve that vision. Tell the universe as specifically as possible what you want it to bring to you and it will absolutely oblige and do so. In Chapter 4 I will get you to look at what you want to attract, and teach you how to use the Law of Attraction to get it. After more than 15 years of personal experimentation, I have chosen the best techniques I have found for manifesting love. These have worked again and again to change people's lives.

Step 4: Build up energy

By asking for help from the spiritual universe, the invisible world of energy around us, we attract energy to our dreams, rather like powering up a rechargeable battery. In Chapter 5 I show you how to work with your dreams at night and also how to relax during the day and use waking dreams to make your vision as real as possible and identify any blocks to manifesting love. Spirit helpers can assist you to open up your heart still further and become a love magnetizer. In Chapters 6 and 7 I show you how to call on help from the spiritual universe. You can ask for help from the energies of the goddesses who are universally connected with love or from your power animal of the heart. You can also build love rituals into your life. You have options here: you can use one or more of these methods. The more belief you have that you can and will attract love, the better your success in doing so. By performing love rituals you tell the universe that your intention is to attract love every single day.

What can you expect to change in your life?

You can expect your life to change to the degree that you believe it is possible to change. The results are entirely dependent on you. I personally believe that you can achieve extraordinary change. I would suggest that it would be helpful for you to believe this, too!

This is a universe of infinite possibilities. It really doesn't matter when you begin your journey, only which path you decide to take. If you make the changes, you will become the change in your own life.

How will you know when you have truly attracted lasting love into your life? Well, there is really only one test and that is the feeling of daily joy – either because you are happy with your own company or have found someone to share your life with.

If you attract a romantic relationship you will find that love starts to fill your life in other ways as well – bringing you more joy, more happiness and more laughter every day, through family and friends as well.

There is a lovely quote from the French writer Henri Nouwen which says it all for me: 'Joy is the experience of knowing that you are unconditionally loved and that nothing – sickness, failure, emotional distress, oppression, war, or even death – can take that love away.'

Is this something you want to experience? Are you ready to be happy in your life? If you can honestly say 'yes', please use this book to help you to reach this daily point of joy by bringing love into your life.

CHAPTER 1

Open to love – the power of thought

'A LOVING HEART IS THE BEGINNING
OF ALL KNOWLEDGE.'

THOMAS CARLYLE

Do you wonder whether you will ever find the true love of someone who will love you for who you are? Do you feel that love may have passed you by?

All of us want love in our lives, whether we admit it or not. It is the most basic human need. If you are ready to free yourself from past hurts, patterns of bad relationships or draining friendships, and ready to bring about a change within your life that will last forever, then I believe that finding love *is* possible, no matter who you are, how old you are and where you live.

However, simply wanting love is not enough to make it come to you. The act of wanting and hoping that something will happen will push it away, as the energy that it gives is the energy of 'lack' (lack of hope, lack of having what you want). In contrast, loving thoughts magnetize love into your life.

In this chapter you will learn:

♥ About the Law of Attraction and the power of thought

♥ How your thoughts attract your future – by intention or default

♥ How to change your thinking and thereby change your life

CASE STUDY: LUCY

Lucy was married for ten years. The first few years when she and her husband Steven were having children together they seemed to be very happy. Lucy stayed at home and brought up the children and Steven went out to work. Then things went wrong. Lucy found out that her husband had been having an affair, not only all the time they had been married, but all the time they had been dating. She was devastated. It took her several months to come to terms with what had happened and to decide what to do because she was scared of being alone and bringing up her children by herself. Eventually, though, Lucy asked Steven to move out.

The whole experience really broke her heart. 'I just felt that I had been so let down by a man that nothing good could ever come of love for me again.' Lucy says now. 'I decided that all men were weak or would betray me in the same way that Steven had. I suppose I also thought deep down that he was so perfect for me that perhaps there was something wrong with me. I just gave up any idea of ever being loved or being happy.'

Lucy had a 'relationship drought period' of over ten years while her children were growing up. She did date from time to time and had a couple of short-lived boyfriends. At the same time she found it very hard to trust any man fully enough to let go and commit to a longer relationship of the type she had had before she met her husband.

'I didn't know that I couldn't commit or trust,' Lucy says. 'If you had asked me over the last few years, I would have said there was nothing I wanted more than someone to fall in love with and to fall in love with me. But part of me never believed it was possible.'

Lucy's story is one that many of us have experienced in similar ways. Once you have been knocked about a bit by an unhappy childhood or a couple of bad love experiences, it is so easy just to let go of the belief that it is possible to find true love. We may long to fall in love but, at the same time, all those old hurts are telling us that we will just get hurt again. If you want to change this pattern then it is important to understand why you attracted these experiences to begin with.

The Law of Attraction

The spiritual way of attracting love is based on the Law of Attraction – the underlying principle of the universe that brings things, events and people into our lives like a magnet. This energetic law, which states that what we attract into our lives is what we give attention to, was known by ancient spiritual traditions as diverse as Polynesian shamanism (spiritual teachings from the islands of the Pacific Ocean, including Hawaii), Tantrism (the esoteric aspect of Hinduism) and the Christian tradition. The knowledge was originally closely guarded by the 'keepers' or 'holy men' of each religion, but has now become widely known.

These traditions all tell of another universe that exists outside the physical, which is referred to as the spiritual universe, in which is found the life force, or creative force.

THE SPIRITUAL UNIVERSE

The universe as a whole is a universe of energy and thought. The energy of the spiritual universe is of a higher frequency of vibration than that of the physical universe, but they are both made up of the same basic material of energy, known by many names: aether, *qi* (*chi*), *mana*, *prana* or simply 'light'. Within the higher frequencies or vibrations of the universe are found spiritual helpers such as angels and other guides (see Chapter 7, page 144). Your higher self, which is your invisible spiritual self, also lives in this part of the universe. Energy carries thought. Every thought you have is alive in the spiritual universe. It is then made real within the physical universe. If you think you will stay healthy, you will. If you believe that you can become rich or attract love, you will. This is the Law of Attraction. To put it simply: what you focus on is what you will create in your life. What you truly believe you are, you will become. The universe is programmed to deliver you the love you want just as soon as you prepare yourself to receive it. It precisely reflects into reality the sum total of everything you believe yourself able to be, do or have.

TRULY BELIEVE

This idea of the universe being programmed to deliver what you want can be confusing. I have had people I have coached say: 'It's not fair. I really want a happy relationship/good friends/more love in my life and I keep thinking about it, but it doesn't happen? Why not?'

There is a very simple answer to this. We attract into our lives *everything* we give attention to, whether it is positive or negative. All of reality exists first in the mind before it exists in your present. So if you spend ten minutes a day consciously thinking about all the loving, happy experiences you are going to bring into your life and then spend the other 23 hours and 50 minutes unconsciously believing that this sort of experience never happens to you, guess which experience you are going to create?

The Law of Attraction works at the level of thought. We draw towards us what we really believe we are deserving of in our lives. If you believe you can find a love who will adore and cherish you, then you will manifest or draw that person into your life in reality. If you don't love yourself at a deep level, then you will unconsciously create experiences in your life that fulfil that belief that you are unlovable.

The universe is aware on a moment-by-moment basis of what you are focusing on. To attract love into your life, pay attention to what you *really* think and *really* believe. It is not enough just to hope and want something to happen. Your life will change at the moment you truly believe it *can* happen and start to imagine a new future.

For the ten or so years when Lucy (see case study on page 14) desperately wanted to bring more love into her life, she didn't succeed because of a tussle going on inside her that she was only partly aware of. Her head said she wanted love, but another part of her had put a great big shield over her heart. Inside, Lucy was afraid of being hurt again and felt that if she let anyone near her, they would betray her in the way Steven had, because 'maybe it was her fault', 'maybe she was unlovable'.

YOU CAN ONLY ACHIEVE WHAT YOU CAN CONCEIVE AND BELIEVE

Lack attracts lack

Perhaps you are reading this book because you feel that in some way your life is missing love. You feel a lack – a gap that needs to be filled. Perhaps you miss the companionship of friends; on a deeper level you may simply miss the feeling of love.

I can think of few worse feelings than the feeling of being alone without hope of change. It is very easy for other people to tell you to keep busy or look on the bright side of life. But how do you actually pull yourself from a place of lack to a place of belief and abundance?

For what you feel right now, if it isn't love, it is most definitely lack:

Crying over your lost relationship is lack.

That feeling when you are by yourself at home in the evening, longing for a phone call or a friend or someone's arms around you, is lack.

Blaming other people for your pain because they have forgotten to ask how you are, or call you or invite you out, is lack.

Thinking that you aren't good enough, or there is something fundamentally wrong with you that pushes love away, is lack.

Are you willing to change?

Are you willing to do what it takes to bring happiness into your life? This is a question someone asked me once, which really struck home. It is the starting point for all change as far as I am concerned.

Really think about the answer. Take a day or so and see what comes into your mind. Because really, let's be honest, sometimes it is much easier not to be happy and to go on doing things the way we have always done them rather than take action and make a change.

What do you do if the answer is 'no'? Well, the first thing to do is accept that this is where you are right now. Self-acceptance is the place where healing starts and ends. Once you have accepted yourself, you can move forward in a positive way to heal your old hurts and replace your old thinking habits with new ones.

What we are consciously aware of thinking about and focusing on is not always what we are really unconsciously focusing on. It may be that you have very clear wants and goals, but they don't happen. Sometimes our real beliefs about life were formed such a long time ago they are now totally outside our awareness, buried deep in our unconscious minds.

If you take the time to explore your beliefs, then you can also change them.

Make a permanent change to your beliefs

Changing your thoughts is the single biggest leverage you have on manifesting or not manifesting what you want. Changing your thoughts is about feeling better. Empowering beliefs let you feel happier because you have more choices about the life that is available to you.

Many people like the idea of manifestation, but think that changing their thoughts will be difficult, so they give up. Let's clear this up. At its very simplest, belief change is just about using your imagination – if you can imagine your life differently, you can make your life different:

Can you imagine being someone who is loved?

Can you imagine being someone who is loving to his or her self?

Can you imagine being someone who is loving to others?

What would your life be like? What would happen differently in your life?

Whatever thoughts these questions sparked off, just decide to let them be a starting point for a new life. Begin to dream about how your life could be different in the future.

COMMON LACK BELIEFS AND LOVE BELIEFS

These are some common lack beliefs about love:

♥ I don't deserve to be loved

♥ There is something wrong with me

♥ I have to be a particular type of person to be loved

♥ Other people get more love than me because they are better or nicer than me in some way

♥ I have to do or achieve something to deserve love

In contrast here are some loving beliefs:

♥ Everybody deserves love

♥ I deserve love just because I am who I am right now

♥ The universe wants me to be loved

♥ There is enough love to go around for everybody

♥ It doesn't matter what has happened to me in the past, I can still be loved now and in the future

♥ I can play my part in creating love by changing the way I think and act

DECONSTRUCTING OLD THINKING HABITS

There is a story often used to illustrate the inherent strength of learned behaviour.

Five monkeys are put in a cage together with a ladder. A banana is hung from the ceiling. However, whenever a monkey climbs up to get the banana all the monkeys get soaked in iced water. So after a while the monkeys learn not to climb the ladder.

Then there is a twist. One of the original monkeys is replaced. The new monkey starts to climb the ladder, but the other monkeys attack him to stop him. After a while this monkey too learns not to climb the ladder. Then another monkey is replaced and the same pattern of behaviour happens. Eventually no original monkeys remain, but nevertheless all the new monkeys have learned not to climb the ladder.

Think about how this relates to real life. Habits and ways of thinking are passed down within an organization, group or family. After a while the people assume the habit without knowing the original reason for it.

You may have lots of ways of thinking you that are not conscious of. Some of these may protect you from harm – just as the monkeys were protected from being sprayed with iced water – but perhaps they also block you. Maybe there are other ways of thinking that would be more useful and still keep you safe from risk. So if you never take risks in love, it may be time to start asking questions. For example:

Why do I act like this? What are the thoughts that underlie my general way of acting?

How do my current beliefs make me feel?

What are the consequences of my current beliefs on me, on others and on my life as a whole?

You don't have to keep thinking or acting in a particular way just because that's what you have always done, or because that's how other people in your family or your friends have always done it.

BECOME A BELIEF DETECTIVE

Bet you didn't realize that you are already a great detective! You have spent much of your life hunting out evidence to support your current beliefs, whatever they are. As we get older we all get really good at this. We notice the things that happen to us that support our current ways of thinking. We cut out the stuff that doesn't support our current ways of thinking. Once you begin to consciously pay attention to your thinking, your unconscious mind will assist you by making you aware of what beliefs act as barriers to receiving love. Then, in order to change what you think, hunt down the evidence to support the new beliefs you want to adopt.

Are you aware what your beliefs about love are? As you read this book make a note of all the thoughts that occur to you about your attitudes to both love and life in general.

Identify your love-attraction blocks

The more you kid yourself as to why you haven't already got the love you want in your life, the more the blocks to love will persist. As soon as you know what your blocks are then you can free yourself. Admit how you really feel about yourself, about love, about your past hurts and your present emotions, your friends, your family and your life. As soon as you accept these feelings, then you are on the path to putting them right. Here's a very easy way to begin.

Over the next few days read something every day about love. Collect magazine articles, look in the newspaper and search online. Read about couples, read about marriage, read about commitment, read about relationships, friendships, parents and children, families or just being together.

As you read anything you can get your hands on, I just want you to begin to notice your thoughts. The aim of this exercise is for you to notice your true reaction to the idea of love and all the ideas connected with it, such as being a couple and marriage. Be really honest with yourself. There is no point pretending that you feel positive towards love, or happy with the idea of being a couple, if you don't. You need to become really clear about your true beliefs.

Are you happy when you read about other people being happy in love? Perhaps you prefer not to read about other people's happiness because it contrasts with your own feelings? This is quite a common feeling for people who don't have the love they want in their life.

What kind of feeling do you get in your body when you hear or see the word 'love'? For example, you might feel a tightness in your chest or a clenching of the stomach when you hear about a couple marrying. Nev, a client of mine who had been through a very difficult divorce, used to find himself unconsciously scratching his finger where his wedding ring used to be. You don't need to try to interpret anything you notice at the moment, simply note down your reaction and any thoughts associated with it.

Now notice your reaction to words such as 'lover', 'boyfriend', 'girlfriend', 'husband', 'wife' and 'relationship', or to any other words that you associate with love.

What thoughts come into your mind? Do you believe in love? Do you think you have to do something to deserve it? Do you have to be a certain person? To have achieved a certain amount? To earn a particular salary?

These sorts of questions may seem absurd to you, or they may prompt some more thinking. We are all different people with different thoughts, and many of us put extraordinary conditions on love.

Notice your thoughts and feelings over the next few days. If any emotions come up from reading about love, just make a note about where you feel them in your body.

Whatever comes up, just softly observe it and don't judge it. You are where you are. The important thing is for you to clarify for yourself whether you have love-attraction blocks in your thinking, beliefs and feeling. The clearer you become in your mind, the faster it is going to be to fix these blocks and the sooner you can start magnetizing the love you want into your life.

HIDDEN BELIEFS

Another way to uncover your hidden beliefs and feelings about love is to look at what is actually happening in your life. Look at the results you get and analyze them as objectively as possible.

Think to yourself: If this situation was happening to someone else, what would I think that person believed about himself or herself? Would he or she have lack beliefs or love beliefs?

CASE STUDY: JODIE

Jodie was a client I worked with over several months. She kept telling me the same story. No matter what happened, it was always the fault of her friends for not being there when she needed them and she had no idea why this kept happening to her.

When we talked about her past, it was clear that this pattern had been running for most of her life since her father had walked out on the family when the children were very young. She had kept deep inside her unconscious a belief that 'people' always rejected her.

This belief had a huge amount of emotion attached to it, so guess what happened? The pattern kept repeating itself as the Law of Attraction brought more of these experiences into her life, proving that what she believed was actually true.

CASE STUDY: MAGGIE

It is very easy to kid yourself about your own thinking. Maggie kidded herself for years. A very smart and attractive woman and a real party girl, Maggie made a big effort to go out almost every night drinking and dancing as she was miserable when she wasn't with someone. But she very seldom managed a relationship that lasted for more than a few weeks. This was despite the fact that she had signed up for several dating sites and had a constant flow of men asking her out.

In fact Maggie could never understand what went wrong, although her friends could all see what wasn't working. Maggie would start off every relationship in the same way – by playing at being happy. Then gradually her real feelings of lack would surface as the mask slipped. Next she would begin to 'need' to know where her man was and want to control him. Then her behaviour would change and she would either play hard to get or settle for crumbs and put up with whatever he threw at her.

All the time Maggie was unconsciously saying to herself: 'This is what I deserve.' You wouldn't know what was going on when you first met her because on the outside she was a cheerful, exciting person, but inside she was desperately trying to control the flow of her life because of her feeling of lack of love.

One day, Maggie decided to stop being that fake party person any more. She started to look at what she was doing that made her feel worse, and at what didn't and what did work. She made an even bigger decision that, whatever happened, she wasn't going to beat herself up any more – that she was going to stay single and become her own lover first and foremost before she tried to become someone else's lover.

As soon as Maggie made that decision to have a love affair with herself she got asked out, by her usual type of man – the one who used to muck her around and let her down and dump her. But this time things were different. Maggie said 'no' – because she had committed to love herself first. Then she said 'no' to another man, too. The more times she said 'no' to the type of man she was accustomed to, the more it made her realize she had been mad to settle all those times in the past for the wrong type of person. Why? Because she really was worth more.

When she finally started to *really* believe that idea, the universe stopped testing her and Glen, a kind and loving man, showed up. At first, she didn't recognize that Glen was special because she had never attracted a man like him to her in the past. However, the good news is that they are now married.

When Maggie really understood her new belief, she got everything she had asked for. In fact she changed both home and job, as it turned out she hadn't been living any of her life in a way that she really liked very much. Now her life is full of love, new friends and, in the last year, a new baby.

Commit to change

As Maggie in the case study discovered, as soon as you really commit to change, the Law of Attraction gets working for you immediately. It brings you experiences to show you how to build love into your life. Make changes on the outside and things will feel different inside you. Decide to change your thinking and your life will change on the outside exactly in tune with how you have changed inside. It is a constant flow.

Things may go through a slightly muddy period as you change, because the universe will sometimes test your commitment to making this change. That's why Maggie got offered the wrong men before getting offered the right one. Be assured, though, that even if things take time to happen, if you truly commit to loving yourself the Law of Attraction will start the process of shaking up your life and bringing in change. Wonderful friends and a wonderful new love really will show up in your life as soon as this change is complete.

Universal mirrors

If you suspect that you have some negative beliefs about love, like Lucy or Maggie in the case studies, but can't quite grasp what they are, there's another simple way to uncover them and play belief detective.

It's easy to check where you are right now in your progress towards your new life just by looking at the 'universal mirrors' around you. The universe is incredibly logical. It provides us with a very useful checklist we can keep an eye on every day.

What are universal mirrors? Well, have you ever noticed that your friends tend to have the same problems as you do? Do you see people around you who are in some way mirroring back to you what you believe to be true about life? For example, you notice that lots of your friends are lonely or unhappy, or have had bad relationship experiences, or get let down a lot. That could make you believe that this must just be what life is like. Actually, life doesn't have to be like that. It is just the universe mirroring back to you what you believe life to be like, in the form of what's happening around you. You'll often notice the mirrors are strongest in the people closest to you.

As soon as you start to really change your beliefs and pay attention to different thoughts and feelings, you'll start to observe very different people coming into your world. You may see a couple in a café being really loving to each other, or a group of friends out having a great time. Perhaps someone you know, who has had a hard time in the past, will suddenly have a breakthrough. Take these as signs of change in your universe.

MY MIRRORS

Think about the people to whom you are closest on a daily basis. What do you think their beliefs are? What do you think they believe to be true about the world? About love? About being in a couple? About being married? About anything else relevant to what you would like to change in your life?

Be honest with yourself. How much of what you have written down could apply to you?

Check and change your beliefs

Let's get some of your beliefs out in the open.

♥ Write down ten things you believe about love, for example:
'I believe I have to change myself to attract love'
'I believe love isn't possible over the age of 35', and so on...

♥ Identify any beliefs that are lack beliefs. Now really think about these beliefs
and challenge them:
Can you think about any circumstances in which these beliefs might not be true?
What beliefs would you like to hold instead?
What sort of person would you be if you changed your beliefs to abundance
beliefs?
What would your life be like?
Is this something you want? If not, what would you like instead?

♥ Think clearly and tweak out any inner conflicts you might have. Write down
what you really feel about the beliefs you identify. Spend time thinking about
how this affects the way you live your life and what you attract into it. What
evidence can you find to support these abundance beliefs?

Mapping beliefs

One trick I have learned from neuro-linguistic programming (NLP) is to map beliefs visually on paper. Write down each belief in turn, then join them together to make a belief tree or flow chart. You can put arrows from one belief to another to show which belief flows out of another belief or gives rise to more than one thought. By doing this you will begin to see patterns – some beliefs are much deeper than others. If you undo a deep belief you will probably undo several other beliefs at the same time. This is because when we accept an idea as a fact, we then go through life looking for evidence to support it and adopt other beliefs as a consequence. If you can get rid of a deep belief, then the whole belief 'cluster' will disappear. This is why it is important to hunt out evidence to undo the deepest beliefs, and indeed to become aware of any that we are not already aware of.

Opposite is an example of a belief tree. It illustrates how a deep, core belief about love can influence conscious beliefs about love.

A BELIEF TREE EXAMPLE

MY CONSCIOUS BELIEFS ABOUT LOVE

MY PARTNER TREATS ME BADLY

I ALWAYS ATTRACT HORRIBLE PARTNERS

MY RELATIONSHIPS FAIL EASILY

I'M NO GOOD AT RELATIONSHIPS

MY CORE BELIEF ABOUT LOVE

I DON'T BELIEVE I AM LOVABLE

Map your belief

MY BELIEF TREE

♥ Draw your belief tree on the biggest piece of paper you can find, or photocopy the template opposite. Draw in as many branches of beliefs as you can find. You will get great satisfaction as you disprove your limiting beliefs, crossing out some of the branches or drawing on fresh branches with new empowering beliefs.

♥ An alternative is to draw or photocopy two trees to begin with – the first is the limiting belief tree, the second is the empowering belief tree. The second tree could contain beliefs you would like to adopt, too.

♥ Place the trees next to each other. I suggest that you put the limiting belief tree on the left or below the empowering belief tree. Because many of us see the future in our mind's eye as running to the right or in front of us. This little visual trick actually works really well to stimulate the unconscious mind.

♥ The Law of Attraction works according to our thoughts, but also according to our emotions connected with these thoughts. If you are clear which emotions are connected with which particular beliefs, then map these as well. You will find that your limiting belief tree contains all sorts of negative emotions. Your empowering belief tree will contain all sorts of positive emotions.

♥ This contrast is a great motivation for the unconscious to change. As you stop and look at each tree, you will notice how much easier and more pleasant it is to look at the empowering tree versus the limiting tree.

♥ Once you have convinced yourself of the need to change, you can begin to look for the evidence that the empowering beliefs are true (for you specifically, as well as generally true) and that they are the best way forward in your life.

♥ If you need extra convincing, then decide to let go of any old family or group patterns and take on board new beliefs that are suitable for who you are now. Remind yourself, for example, that it might be ridiculous to carry on the same way of thinking about the world as your great-grandparent who lived in a different century.

MY CONSCIOUS BELIEFS ABOUT LOVE

MY CORE BELIEF ABOUT LOVE

IN ESSENCE

It doesn't matter where you are right now. You may have a terrible past record with relationships. You may have had no relationships. You may have had great relationships in the past, but are just not meeting anyone right now. You may hate yourself at times. You may feel lonely or simply bored. You may feel that there is no one else in the world who has quite the same mix of emotions and circumstances as you. It really doesn't matter what has happened up to now in your life. It doesn't matter what kind of relationship you want. It doesn't matter if you are a man or a woman, young or old. The starting point to attract love into your life is precisely where you are right now. The past is the past. The future is a new chapter waiting to be written as you read this guide and begin to put some of what you learn into practice.

As you carry on reading, just begin your new future by starting to become aware of your thought patterns. It is very simple. Pay attention softly to the kind of thoughts you have. Begin to notice when you catch your thoughts from time to time, where you are thinking thoughts of lack rather than loving and abundant thoughts. When you catch yourself in lack, just make a mental note. There is no need to tell yourself off or anything else. For the moment just be aware.

MY NOTES

CHAPTER 2

Heal your past

'KEEP WALKING, THOUGH THERE'S NO PLACE
TO GET TO. DON'T TRY TO SEE THROUGH THE
DISTANCES. THAT'S NOT FOR HUMAN BEINGS.'

RUMI

♥

In this chapter you will learn ways in which to heal negative emotions connected to your past relationships. Negative emotions can get in the way of attracting love as the vibration of anger, guilt or sadness is stored at a cellular level in your body. Negative emotions remain as blocks in your unconscious, causing you to attract the same old patterns and people until they are healed and cleared away.

There are many different ways to heal your past. You can use spiritual rituals, meditation, neuro-linguistic programming (NLP), trance, body work or magical techniques. They are all designed to do one thing – stop you filling your energy with 'lack' (see page 18) caused by negative thinking so that you create a space for positivity, laughter, fun, joy and, of course, love attraction.

In this chapter you will learn:

♥ What your love résumé can teach you

♥ How to identify the roles you play in your life and to let go of unhelpful past roles

♥ How to heal hurt and the Hawaiian practice of forgiveness – a method you can use to help yourself heal

CASE STUDY: CHRISTINA NOBLE

A woman whose story I greatly admire is Christina Noble. Christina was born in Ireland to a poor family. Her father was an alcoholic and when Christina was ten she was left on the streets of Dublin, caring for her brother and sister, before being sent to an orphanage. She lived there until the age of 16, when once again she was forced to care for herself.

Christina wrote about this horrific childhood in her beautiful autobiography *Bridge Across My Sorrows*. Many young people growing up with hardship and poverty and no family support might give up on life, or turn to drugs or alcohol and re-create the family patterns over the generations. Christina was different. She had a dream, about as distant as possible from her daily troubles in Ireland. She dreamed of helping suffering children in Vietnam, prompted by the Vietnamese war. Extraordinarily, Christina did something about this dream. In 1989,

she travelled to Vietnam and began to help Vietnamese street children.

In time, she set up the Christina Noble Children's Foundation, which has grown over the last decades and now helps children in Mongolia as well as Vietnam. The foundation has set up schools, clinics and shelters, even soccer teams and music lessons. I went to her centre in Ho hearMin (Saigon) in Vietnam during the early 1990s, and met some of the children who were being loved and cared for by Christina.

Christina is an amazing person, who exemplifies how it is possible to heal your past and change not only your own life, but also the lives of others. She has brought love to thousands of other lives and is immensely loved herself.

If you feel controlled by your past, you needn't be. By using some of the techniques described in this chapter you can start to change the way your future is formed.

Fear of change

Some people have only one fear, and that is fear of change. Even though they haven't got exactly what they want in life, and they aren't comfortable, they aren't too *uncomfortable*. They fear, for example, that because having a relationship hurt them in the past, it might hurt again, so by not trying to attract love at least they can avoid misery.

There's a story that relates how there was a man who was afraid of lots of things. He was worried that the earth would collapse and swallow him up. He was afraid that the sky would collapse one day and fall on top of him. The more and more he thought about all the things that could happen to him, the more he worried. It got to the point when he was too afraid to sleep in case something terrible happened while he was in bed. Then a friend took him aside and explained that he could keep living in fear if he wanted to, but really his fears were groundless. He explained that earth is just dirt and the sky is just air. Air is light and couldn't hurt him. The earth had never cracked. Why should it crack now?

It is easy to imagine all the things that can happen that are bad, but why bother? Why not simply forget about those possibilities, change focus and work out what you want to bring into your life instead that is happy and fun and exciting and loving?

You always have the choice, no matter what, to refuse to be ruled by fear, guilt, blame or any other negative emotion you have learned. You were born a loving creature who was meant to be a love attractor. Babies assume they will be loved and looked after. There is no need for you as an adult to be any different. You were once a natural love attractor. You can and will be again. You can take a practical step forward through your fear by looking at your past so you can heal it.

Your love résumé

Writing a love résumé is a good place to start. A résumé is a way of tweaking out any thoughts about love within relationships. It serves several purposes. It is a summary of your past experience and it shows all your skills and achievements.

You may already have a career résumé – something you typically sit down and write only when you are ready to move on to another job. You sit down and work out what skills you have that your future employer might want. Well, a love résumé isn't that different. It's a way of thinking about all your past experiences and learning from them so that you can move forward to something better in the future. In the same way you have to think about your career, writing a love résumé gives you the opportunity to think about everything you want to keep in your life and everything you want to discard.

What does your love résumé look like? A little patchy? Full of lovely experiences and people you have met in the past? Or does it contain some experiences that you would rather not repeat in the future?

Unlike your career résumé, you're not going to show your love résumé to anyone, but it is going to help you to change your future relationships as long as you write everything down. A written love résumé lets you be very objective about what has and hasn't worked in the past.

Write a love résumé

♥ Jot down on a piece of paper a list of all the relationships you have had up to now. Write down the specifics, times and dates.

♥ Then take a long look at what you have written. Notice what sort of situations and people you have attracted to you in the past. Perhaps you have some themes running through your résumé? If so, make a note of what you think they are.

♥ Write down any beliefs that you think you would like to change. You can use the belief change process in Chapter 1 (see pages 20–31) to challenge and change these.

♥ Next think about yourself in relation to these relationships. What beliefs and ways of thinking in you attracted these relationships to you? Remember that the Law of Attraction works on a 'like attracts like' principle.

♥ Now look at your experiences in the past. Just as you would if you were thinking about your career, be objective. There will be some things you have experienced in the past that you would like to experience again:
What do you want to keep?
What characteristics of the person in the past, or your life together, worked for you?

♥ Make a separate list of the features of relationships that you would like to keep in the next relationship you have – and perhaps have even more of.

CASE STUDY: DAVE

A client, Dave, had gone through a very painful divorce, which he had taken five years to get over. He wanted to make sure that when he started a new relationship he changed the ways he had done things in the past.

Dave had two big themes running through his love résumé. He attracted very stable women who wanted to settle down with him quickly, in which case he cut the relationship off within weeks, or he found himself pursuing women who were exciting and beautiful, but generally already in some sort of complicated situation with another man. He hadn't realized he had this pattern of behaviour until he saw it starkly in front of him on paper.

So what was the common universal mirror (see page 30) in his résumé? What Dave realized after a while was that none of the women in his life really loved themselves. Either they wanted a relationship and were needy because they didn't feel OK with themselves, or they were unavailable because they didn't want people getting too close to them. Dave recognized that he had behaved in the same way in his marriage. He and his wife had played cat and mouse with each other for years, but when he hit a bad spot in his life and needed real love the marriage didn't survive. After creating his love résumé Dave realized that what he needed in his life was a relationship that was very different – and truly loving.

44

Think in positive language

Having done your love résumé, it is important from now on to focus on what worked rather than what didn't work, so that you can attract more of what you want. The Law of Attraction doesn't process negatives. If you think, 'I don't want rejection', it hears the word 'rejection' and brings you more of it. Instead of thinking, 'I don't want any more of a man/woman who forgets to give me presents', turn your thinking around and say to yourself: 'I liked the fact he/she remembered my birthday. Now I would like even more fun, shared hobbies, romantic evenings together, Sunday dinners, intelligent talk, laughter and presents', then you will start attracting more abundance into your life.

Identify the roles you play

True love is unconditional. Unconditional love is abundant. It frees you up to have choices in your life. When you are in a really loving relationship, you will feel more of yourself, not less of yourself. However, holding on to negative feelings results in us playing roles rather than letting love flow freely. Look back at your love résumé. How many of the following roles, if any, have you played in the past?

ROLE ONE – THE JUDGE

Your inner judge is the part of you that passes sentence on you. You'll know if you have an inner judge because it will tell you that you are not good enough, a bad person and not worthy, and will sentence you to the punishment of a life without unconditional love.

A judge is unforgiving, not only of self, but also of others. If you feel very bad about yourself you may find that you are very harsh about other people as well, as a way of deflecting attention from yourself.

However, as the old saying goes: 'one finger points out, three fingers point back'. If you pass judgement on other people you get it back threefold. If you pass love to other people you get it back threefold. Whatever we project to the world we receive back. If you are judging the behaviour of other people it is because inside you feel a victim.

ROLE TWO - THE VICTIM

The victim is the part of you who thinks events and other people are responsible for what happens to you in life. A victim feels powerless and helpless. A victim doesn't feel they have the freedom to choose their own life.

A love victim attracts relationships where other people dump them or treat them badly. They do not feel they have the power to show themselves as they really are because they are afraid of bullying, abuse and attack.

I am sure you have met a number of victims in your life. You may even have been one yourself on occasion. Yes, I know it's embarrassing to admit it, but many of us do like sympathy when we have ended a relationship or during a relationship. The trouble is that while we may get a bit of sympathy, we don't get love. This is not a love-attraction pattern that works because it is founded on lack beliefs rather than loving beliefs.

If you are a victim, then you lack one thing in addition to love and that is hope. The part of you that is a victim feels not worthy to receive love. It feels in some way to blame for the fact that it can't receive the love it wants. So it doesn't expect that things will change. The Law of Attraction works on expectation, so if any part of you is a victim experiencing these feelings, then you won't attract love to you.

If you are still not sure whether you have adopted the victim role in the past, then think about these questions:

> *Do you blame yourself for the fact that you haven't attracted the love you want into your life so far?*

> *Do you feel guilty that you aren't good enough in some way?*

> *Do you feel ashamed about anything and therefore feel unworthy of real love?*

If you say 'yes' to any of these questions, then you are playing out victim lack patterns in your life. The beliefs that underlie the 'yes' are all untruths.

CASE STUDY: EVIE

Evie really demonstrated again and again the effect that playing victim can have on your life. She had had a series of one-year relationships over a ten-year period. They never lasted longer than that.

At the end of each relationship she ended up telling me what terrible things her boyfriends had done to her. The relationship had never just 'not worked out'. There was the boyfriend who spent all her money. There was the boyfriend who had an affair. Then there was the boyfriend who slapped her across the face during an argument. Whoever she met, the pattern was the same. They behaved badly and she was the victim.

She finally met a man whom her friends all liked but Evie said he was the most selfish man she had ever met. The relationship ended and Evie was alone again. Who did she blame? She blamed him of course. She felt that she was the victim and again and again she attracted the same relationship pattern to her because her beliefs about herself didn't change.

Letting go of judge and victim

It is time to let go of self-judgement once and for all. Judging yourself, blaming yourself and feeling guilty all destroy the love magnet within you because they destroy self-acceptance.

The less you beat yourself up, the more you accept yourself and the more love you feel. The more love you feel, the more lovable you become.

Do you deserve love? The only true answer here is 'yes'. We all deserve love. We are all worthy of love. We are all good enough. We are all born to receive unconditional love. If you feel that something inside you is not deserving of love, it is a lie that you have learned. Healing all the hurts you have carried from the past lets you live your life so that your love begins to expand.

Healing the hurt – feel the feelings and let go

Just stop for a moment. Notice, if you are carrying negative feelings, where they are in your body. This is something I first learned from Tibetan Buddhism, but it has been taken up by non-spiritual practitioners such as exponents of neuro-linguistic programming as well. When you feel an emotion you may feel it as a tightness, a change in temperature, or even as a moving feeling within your stomach, chest or another part of your body.

Think about fear. Think about blame or guilt. Where are you carrying these emotions? Feelings have a texture to them, they carry an energy charge that can be felt as hot or cold. You feel a feeling because it is an energy within the cells of your body. Each time you express the pain you do so in order to make it go away, but instead it actually makes it stay – stored in your body.

Next time you start feeling that you are a judge or victim and notice all the negative emotions that come out of those patterns of behaviour, think about how you are carrying all those emotions in your body and what they are doing to you:

♥ Instead of beating yourself up, simply say: 'No one is to blame here' and let it go.

♥ Instead of feeling guilty for not being perfect, simply say: 'Well, no one is perfect, so who cares. I am fine as I am.'

♥ Instead of pointing the finger at the boyfriend or girlfriend who didn't behave in the way you hoped or expected, simply say: 'They did the best they could at the time and so did I.'

♥ Instead of saying: 'There must be something wrong with me or things would have worked out better', simply say: 'Who cares' or 'There's always a next time'.

♥ Instead of saying: 'He/she is a bad person', simply say: 'This is what I did love about them. This is what I learned from the experience and this is what I am going to ask for more of next time.'

♥ Instead of punishing yourself as a judge so that you can play the victim, forgive yourself. Be kind. We spend so much time beating ourselves up that we often forget to be kind. Relax. Let it go.

FORGIVENESS

Ask the universe what you need to learn from the experiences you have had in the past. If there is pain or loss or hurt, then ask what you need to learn to let go of these feelings.

Forgive your past boyfriends.

Forgive your past girlfriends.

Forgive the friends who have hurt you.

Forgive your parents.

Forgive yourself.

Evie, in the case study on page 48, kept refusing to forgive her past boyfriends because she said if she forgave them, they would 'get away with it' – get away with not having treated her well – and it wouldn't be 'fair'. But the only one suffering was Evie. Even though it may seem unfair to forgive, ultimately every time you forgive another person you are actually helping yourself. On an energetic level we are all joined together. The image of another person you carry inside you with all those negative feelings attached to it is part of you. When you forgive that person, you get rid of the negative energy within yourself. Forgiveness is the easiest path to love. Every time you forgive yourself, you bless those cells in your body that were filled with pain. You allow them to leave your body. You thank them for how they have served you and then you let go.

Every time you let go of a bad experience and move on, you clear out pain and hurt and make space for love.

Hawaiian practices of love and forgiveness

Before other people will show you love, you must discover your own self as a hidden treasure. The ritual below is a wonderful way of beginning this process.

I first visited Hawaii 15 years ago to study Hawaiian shamanism, a spiritual tradition that is possibly 35,000 years old. Some people believe that the islands of Hawaii are equivalent to the seven chakras of our planet (see page 69), acting as core energy points for the Earth. In Hawaii shamans are known as *kahunas* – a name that originally probably meant a master or doctor and evolved to mean a priest or magician. Over the years *kahunas* have been psychics, healers and even shamans who were said to be able to influence the weather.

The ancient teachings of Hawaii are known as 'Huna', which translates as 'the secret'. It is likely that much of Huna wisdom is still secret, as different Huna traditions were guarded within the islands and lineages of Hawaii. It is only relatively recently that Huna has been studied outside the islands and become more open within them.

HAWAIIAN FORGIVENESS RITUAL

Huna teaches that one of the most important things you can do is to practise forgiveness. This isn't a new message. Forgiveness is key to every great spiritual tradition, but within the Huna tradition forgiveness is part of what is known as the Huna Prayer, a method of manifesting. Forgiving others, preferably as a daily practice, is actually a way of forgiving yourself and of self-healing.

Huna can also be translated to mean the perfect balance of feminine and masculine, or yin and yang. *Hu* means masculine and *na* feminine. Every Huna practice brings the two poles together and ourselves into balance. In Huna the forgiveness practice is known as *ho' o' pono pono*, which means 'to make things right/balanced' (*pono*). The practice of forgiveness heals you energetically and brings you into balance. A balanced person is full of self-love and ready to attract love from everyone, including from a romantic partner.

LOVE AND HARMONY

The ancient Hawaiians understood that in order to attract love we need first to be happy and healed within ourselves. You can't participate in a loving relationship with another person if you can't love yourself.

Love and harmony are inseparable in the Huna spiritual tradition. The word for love in Hawaiian is *aloha*. *Ha* means the breath of life, *alo* means to be with and *oha* means happiness. Together these sounds are used as a loving welcome because the ancient Hawaiians greeted others with love. When you say *aloha* to someone you are telling them you want to share happiness and joy with them. Spiritually, you understand that everything you do touches someone else. Your energy directly attracts other energies of the same vibration. If you have inner happiness you will magnetize happy people towards you. You won't need to seek out love; it will naturally be drawn towards you by your energy.

ENERGETIC CORDS

Every time you make a connection with someone you send an energetic cord from your energy body towards them. A connection is any kind of contact, including a simple thought about that other person or any kind of emotional connection. You have energy cords to and from people you are related to, including ancestors, people you are friends with, people you work with and people you have loved or had intimate relations with. Sometimes it is useful to disconnect and reconnect with these people, or simply to disconnect the cords so that you establish new relationships with them. After you have disconnected, you will find that your relationship feels very different to both of you – always in a positive way, when you have done this process lovingly.

Perform the Hawaiian forgiveness ritual

The process of *ho' o' pono pono* ('Making things right') is very simple. It is something you can do on a daily basis.

♥ Simply sit somewhere you won't be distracted and quieten your mind.

♥ Imagine that you have a small stage in front of you. You can call on to that stage anyone from your life that you have unresolved issues with – perhaps ex-lovers or family members. Anybody whose image you hold in your mind with anger or grief, or any other negative emotion, is a drain on your inner love and happiness.

♥ Hold these images in your mind's eye on your stage with love. The easiest way to do this is to surround them with the white loving light of the universe. The energy of the universe vibrates with infinite love and healing. 'Infinite' means that the love will never be scarce. There is enough to heal anything.

♥ Imagine the top of your head (the crown chakra, see page 69) opening up to let this loving healing light flow down through your whole body, filling it up so much that it pours out through your heart on to the people on the stage, filling them with love and healing.

♥ Say what you need to say to them. Hear what they need to say to you. Forgive them in your mind and thank them for what they have given you. Hear them forgive you for the unwitting projections or harm you have done to them.

♥ If you find this difficult, just remember that the people you see in your mind's eye are part of you. These images are in your unconscious, and holding on to any negative feelings only harms you. Forgiving others and letting go of these feelings is really a process of forgiving yourself for the experiences you went through. Let go and you will lift the dark spots in your unconscious, making way for light and joy and love.

♥ When you have completed the forgiveness process, say thank you to the people on the stage. Imagine a scythe of white light cutting the energetic cords that have kept you bound to each other. Let the cords return to whom they belong, bringing back to you all the energy that has been wasted on negativity so that it is transmuted into love and light once again. Then the people are free to leave.

♥ If the images are of people who are still in your life, this doesn't necessarily mean that you have to let go of contact with those people. Any time you think of them again you restore a connection with them. However, because you have let go of the negative energies, the fresh connection will be lighter, more loving and more balanced than before.

♥ You can repeat this process as often as you like and you will find it gets easier and easier. It clears the path of any blocks to manifesting the life you want, including the love you want.

'BE PATIENT TOWARDS ALL THAT IS UNRESOLVED IN YOUR HEART. LEARN TO LOVE THE QUESTIONS THEMSELVES.'
RAINER MARIA RILKE

IN ESSENCE

You don't need to play roles any more in your relationships. Playing a role, being victim or judge, won't get you the relationship you both want or truly do deserve to have. Importantly it isn't a way of attracting love to you. Playing a role may get you some short-term sympathy, but it will also drive other people away.

Love is attracted by you being your true self – the perhaps vulnerable, but certainly lovable you.

You don't need to be ruled by what has happened to you in the past. Instead you can choose to let go of any bad feelings you have about your past. You can let go of bad feelings about past relationships, past friendships that have hurt you and any other past hurts. By forgiving what has happened to you in the past and taking charge of how you focus on your past, you will start to feel differently. You will create different energy around you and a space into which love can flow once more.

You can use the techniques in this chapter to help you to heal any past hurts. By doing this you will banish negative patterns of behaviour and create a fresh, energetically neutral starting point from which to begin to manifest a different and loving future.

MY NOTES

CHAPTER 3

Fall in love with yourself

'YOU, YOURSELF, AS MUCH AS ANYBODY IN
THE ENTIRE UNIVERSE, DESERVE YOUR
LOVE AND AFFECTION.'

BUDDHA

♥

When you make changes in your everyday life on a practical level you will start to feel differently about yourself; your body language will change, the things you say will change. When you change on the inside, people will begin to react differently to you and the experiences you attract into your life will change. Learning to love yourself is a vital step towards attracting love from others into your life.

In this chapter you will learn:

♥ About the key belief that supports love

♥ How to dance on the inside: love your body, your mind and the inner you

♥ How to open your heart chakra and give love to the world

♥ About heart-to-heart cords and the difference between sex and love

Love yourself first

I often meet people who are baffled as to why they haven't attracted loving friends or a loving partner into their life. 'I am such a nice person,' they say. 'Look at that person over there. They are not nearly as nice as me. I help people out, I do good deeds. I am always helpful to others, so why don't people ring me up or invite me out? Why don't I have a special person in my life who loves me?' If you put other people first without really loving yourself at the same time, you won't attract lasting love. The Law of Attraction acts on a 'like attracts like' basis, so the people who come into your life will have the same issues about love as you.

When you don't love yourself, then you can't really love another person. Instead you feel an addiction or a need to be with that person, to know what they are doing and to control their actions so that they can't leave you.

The key love belief

There is one belief that people who attract love easily have about themselves: 'I am perfect just as I am.'

The truth is we are all born perfect. You just need to look at yourself and recognize that fact. We are all born to be loved. You don't need to do anything to attract other people to you, other than recognize the love within yourself.

Love doesn't come by you trying to force it or by you striving to make it happen. Love is already there inside you. It reveals itself when you begin to nourish yourself. All manifestation in the material world starts by you working on yourself on the *inside*. You will only create change externally when you have first created change internally.

How much do you love yourself? If you don't love yourself, how can you expect others to fall in love with you?

In this chapter I am going to show you how to embark on a journey of self-discovery to fall in love with yourself so that you can open your heart to receiving more love from others. The secret really is so simple: love yourself and you will attract love.

Change happens when you love the whole of you – inside and outside. So let's look at some steps you can take.

BECOME ENTRANCING

Have you ever noticed any of these things happening to you when you are in love?

♥ You notice wonderful details about another person or the world around you

♥ Time feels as if it is passing at a different rate

♥ Your senses become heightened – the world feels and looks richer and more vibrant, perhaps more exciting

If the answer is 'yes', it's because you are in a love trance. In a love trance we cut out all the negative 'chatter' around us and focus only on the good things. It is a wonderful feeling – like going around in your own blissful little bubble.

When we fall in love we become entranced by the person we are in love with. We find everything about them delightful, even mesmerizing. I have chosen my words very carefully here. The word 'mesmerizing' comes from the name of the physician, Franz Mesmer, who theorized in the late 18th/early 19th century about mesmerism, the forerunner of hypnosis. He was able to put people into a trance through just his words and actions. When you are in a trance you are in a different state, noticing different things about yourself or other people than you would in your normal state of mind. If you have ever seen people on stage in a hypnosis show, you'll have seen very clearly how they can be guided to behave differently from usual. I am not suggesting that you need believe that you are a chicken, or go and do a headstand against the wall, as you may have seen in a hypnosis show, but do something much more useful – become entranced by yourself!

Actually, if you have ever tried any form of meditation or self-hypnosis, or any other kind of trance induced by shamanistic drumming or deep-breathing practices like rebirthing, you will recognize these descriptions of being entranced. The word 'entrance' makes you think of 'being delightful, wonderful and beautiful to yourself and others' as well as 'being in a trance'. When you go into a trance state you can create the love vibration that will not only make you notice all the good things about yourself, but will also attract love from other people.

What I want to happen to you while you read this book is that you fall deeply in love with yourself. Be open to the possibility that it could happen quite quickly, if not suddenly out of the blue, because that is how love often strikes. You'll know when it has happened because you will start to dance on the inside. You will feel a sense of joy about yourself that will feel strangely familiar, really because it is not new but just remembering what you were born to believe about yourself.

LOVE THE INNER 'YOU' BEHIND THE MASK

There is a Buddhist tale about the man who goes searching for happiness. No matter where he looks he can't find it because it has been hidden in the one place we always forget to look – deep inside ourselves.

We all have masks. A mask is the identity we show to the world and to ourselves. Sometimes we are aware that we are putting on a mask and sometimes we are not. Sometimes we forget we are wearing masks and think we are that person.

Many of us do this when we are embarking on a new relationship because, if we haven't had much luck in the past, we think we have to pretend to be someone different to win our date over.

Have you ever walked into a party and put on a false front? Have you ever been on a date and pretended to be interested in things you weren't, or be someone you aren't?

The trouble with this approach is that you won't be able to keep it up for very long. When you let the mask slip, your date will realize that you are a different person and that's often too much of a shock. Then, if the date goes wrong, you think it's because you showed yourself. Actually it is because you didn't show yourself early enough.

When you really love yourself from the inside there is no need to wear a big mask any more. Be who you are. I don't care if you are a little whacky or a bit unusual or slightly geeky. It really doesn't matter if you are so lazy that you get up late every day, or like collecting newts, or never pick the clothes up off your floor or wear the same pants three days in a row. Honestly, there is someone out there who won't care. There are probably lots of people out there who won't care. More than that, they will actually love you even more because you have a few peculiarities and differences.

In some of the happiest couples I have seen, one or both people are a little bit grumpy, or unsocial or different in another way. Yet the more you get to know them, the more you realize how attractive this honesty is.

CASE STUDY: TOM

Tom married a girl who was one of the most straight-talking – almost rude – people his friends had ever met. They all wondered what on earth he was doing. He knew so many other girls. But you know what? He knew exactly what he was doing.

She was up front and honest and straight down the line, and the more all his friends got to know her, the more they understood. There was no gossip with her, or lying to make people feel better when something wasn't going well. The result was everyone knew exactly where they were with her. It made her really easy to be with because 'she was who she was'.

Authenticity is one of the most potent aphrodisiacs in the world because it lets you show your vulnerability to your potential partner. If you consistently pretend to be someone you are not in order to attract love, you will only attract lack. This is because the belief that underlies a mask is that the real person inside isn't good enough to show to the world. Trust enough that you are perfect to show yourself from the outset.

LOVE THE OUTER YOU

Many of us spend too much time every day thinking about what's wrong with us on the outside. This isn't helped by the media, which talk about celebrities' appearances obsessively, commenting on the slightest pimple, sign of baldness or cellulite as if the poor person in question has committed a terrible sin by not conforming to some abstract idea of perfection. It's therefore not surprising if you look at yourself in the mirror occasionally and feel dissatisfied.

However, from a Law of Attraction point of view, this isn't a helpful thing to do. All those people out there in the world who are reading magazines and comparing themselves with some airbrushed celebrity are operating out of lack.

Of course, all of us do it from time to time – think we aren't pretty enough, are too fat or too thin, have the wrong colour of hair, are of the wrong height or the wrong age. It seems quite harmless, doesn't it? But it isn't really. After all, you wouldn't tell children that they are ugly. You wouldn't tell children that they need to dye their hair, or have a nose operation. You would probably even think it abusive if you caught an adult telling a child these things not just once, but every day, or even several times a day? I would, yet I have to admit I say things to myself that I would never dream of saying to a child. The truth is, when I look at young children, whatever they look like I really only notice how perfect they are.

In reality, the majority of faces are fascinating. Yes, bodies come in all shapes and sizes and some of us have more wrinkles than others, but does that make us less perfect? The more I have thought about this over the years, the more I notice how you can find beauty in anybody at any age.

I was once told by a film director the secret of why we love Hollywood stars. It's because the camera lingers over every feature. It doesn't matter whether the star is youthful or an older character actor. The camera allows us to look at their faces close up, lingering on each of them. The only other time we get to look at someone that closely for that long is if the other person is your lover, child or parent. In other words, the reason we find these stars so fascinating to look at is because the camera gives us permission to look at them properly and thus we discover we love them. We love every imperfection, every little bit of their face. It's such a mesmeric process that just by looking at an actor in this way can redefine our views on beauty. A star like Gerard Depardieu is probably a case in point. By staring at his unusual features again and again we begin to notice that these kinds of features are as compellingly attractive as daintier, more uniform features.

So next time you catch sight of yourself in the mirror, linger a while. Give yourself the attention you would give to a face in a movie. Let yourself notice how fascinating each part of your face and body is. Become entranced with yourself in the way you become entranced with a lover you are with for the first time.

Begin to love your life

Think about what makes you happy in life generally. What makes you feel alive? What makes you laugh? What brings you joy?

If you have been in the habit of focusing on what doesn't make you happy – all that lack and loneliness and discomfort from not feeling loved enough – it takes some retraining to keep feeling happy on a daily basis.

Acknowledging and starting to let go of 'wrong thinking' as we have already explored is a great place to begin. Actually taking action to *do* more things you enjoy every day will accelerate your progress and bring your focus more and more towards joy. Every time you feel happy and light in yourself, you raise your energy vibration and begin to attract better and better experiences towards you.

TIP THE HAPPINESS BALANCE

Think about your average day at the moment. What do you do? Get up at a certain time? Eat breakfast, lunch and an evening meal? Go to work? Watch TV? Or stay at home? If you don't have love in your life right now, then it is time to inject a bit of joy and excitement into your routine.

Often it is having too much of a routine that is the issue itself. We all need a bit of change and excitement and spontaneity to shake us up from time to time. Sameness and structure are great supports for people, but we'd all still be living in caves if it wasn't for difference and change.

What could you do that would be fun, spontaneous, maybe a bit daring? Of course it depends on the person and how daring their life is to begin with. Take some people I know: Lydia craved a big adventure after her divorce, so one day she took off to South America to work for a charity for three months; Nicki decided to take up dancing even though, at the age of 60, she had thought she was a bit old to do anything new; Janet's new fun activity was staying in on a Friday night and cooking for girlfriends.

It really doesn't matter what other people think. The point is that you decide how much of a change to your routine is going to shake things up and tip the happiness balance in your favour.

What do you want to do? Run around the park playing with your dog, set off on a round-the-world trip, take up belly dancing, go and see live comedy, make homemade chocolates, write a book, lie in the sun or just get out of your chair and move more?

80/20

Make a list of the top things that you love. I always work on the 80/20 principle. If you do the most important 20 per cent regularly, then you will tip your happiness balance in your favour by 80 per cent. You don't have to do everything on the list, just the things that make the biggest difference.

If you are still not sure what to do, make a promise to yourself to lighten up. Let go of all the unimportant stuff in your life. Don't cling on to hurts.

Remember always to have a sense of humour. If on the odd occasion – and let's face it, all of us have them – you can't manage to laugh in the face of bad luck or a dull day, keep curious. That will always direct your mind away from what you don't want and towards what you do. Always maintain a joyful mind.

There is only one measure of your success and that's how you feel. As soon as you begin to feel lighter, to feel happier, to feel more excited, to feel calmer, to feel that you enjoy your life more, it is working.

Every time you catch yourself having this feeling of loving your life, then it is going to make you into a love-attraction magnet, feeling more and more love as if the happiness in you is calling out across the universe to lovers and friends to come into your life *now*.

Opening your heart

If you have been living in lack for a while you may have constructed energetic defences around your heart.

Your heart chakra (see pages 69–70) needs to be able to open up freely to attract love. Sometimes our chakras get blocked. If you look at a Kirlian, or energy, photograph of a person, you can see that someone who is emotionally and spiritually balanced has clear, beautifully coloured chakras going in a straight line up the front of the body. In a person who is unhappy, depressed or unbalanced in another way, some of these colours may be barely visible. Some chakras may be much more dominant than others. A balanced, loving heart looks pink or green. When it is open, the energy swirls around and looks like a bright flower opening up.

If you are not experiencing either receiving or giving love easily, then take the time to focus on the health of your heart chakra. This is a really simple process and you can spend just a few minutes on it whenever you remember.

CHAKRAS

The word 'chakra' comes from Sanskrit and means a wheel. It generally refers to the seven energy centres, which regulate the flow of energy through and around the human body. The seven chakras are each associated with a different colour and are located on a point that corresponds to a part of the physical body (see diagram below).

Chakras are part of the energy system, which keeps us healthy not just on a physical level, but also on an emotional, spiritual and mental level. When a chakra is healthy and balanced, we are healthy. If the flow of energy within the chakra is disturbed, you will find that you become ill or affected negatively in some way on a physical or other level.

If you have suffered a lot of hurt in love, this will affect the balance of your chakras and can be detected by someone with psychic skills.

Learning to open and close your chakras at will is part of the meditation practices in this book, which will help you learn to attract love into your life.

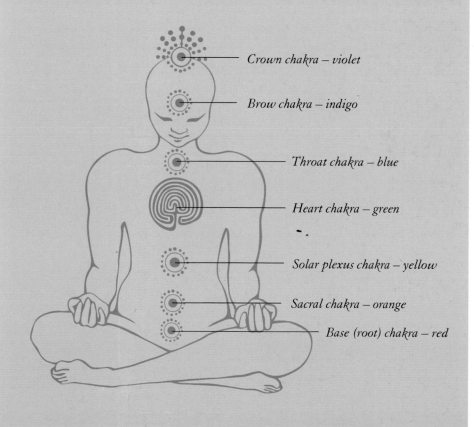

Crown chakra – violet

Brow chakra – indigo

Throat chakra – blue

Heart chakra – green

Solar plexus chakra – yellow

Sacral chakra – orange

Base (root) chakra – red

Open up your heart chakra

♥ Imagine that your heart chakra is like a flower with petals that can open or close. Eastern traditions use the lotus as a symbol.

♥ See in your mind's eye the petals of the flower opening to receive all the love that is out there in the universe, and also to give love. When you give, though, see energy flowing down through the top of your head and your crown chakra and out through your heart, so that you always draw on universal energy, which never runs out.

♥ Then use this image from a Buddhist-derived tradition called 'heart yoga'. Imagine that you have a diamond, a most precious thing. See the diamond in the lotus of your heart and feel its joy and beauty. Let it stay there, radiating beauty and love. Let it radiate love out towards you, filling your whole energy body with love. Let it radiate love out towards the world. Know that there is always enough love to draw upon any time it is needed.

FLOW YOUR LOVE TO THE UNIVERSE

When your love for yourself is full, there will always be enough for you to give out to the universe. Compassion for other people is held up in many spiritual traditions as a integral part of being a loving person. Giving love abundantly boosts your energetic link with the flow of love in the universe. It reminds you that love is an energy to be shared and that we all deserve.

There is a traditional way of thinking in Tibetan Buddhism that teaches you to be compassionate by suggesting that you treat all people as your parent. When you walk around, look at strangers and thin: This person is my mother or my father. Take a look at the people you come into contact with every day. Look at the woman on the bus who is having an argument about the fare and holding you up when you are in a hurry. Can you think of her as your mother? Look at the man on the news who robbed a shop. Can you think of him as your father? Look at your neighbours who keep you awake at night playing loud music. Can you think of them as your parents?

All the great spiritual traditions tell us that we are not separate from other people, but connected. When you send out love to other people it comes back to you.

Heart cords

As we have already discussed in Chapter 2 (see page 53), every time you think about someone, an energetic cord extends from your energy body to the other person. Likewise when they think about you, an energy cord extends from them to you. Where in the energy body the link happens is key to what it feels like.

When you love another person with your heart, you send out an energetic cord from your heart to their heart. This love empowers both of you. It feels intimate and permissive and non-judgemental.

This is very different from love that comes from need or co-dependence. If you could actually see energetic cords and looked at two people bound together through need rather than love, then you would literally see the binding. The energetic cords between them wouldn't be a straight cord from heart to heart, but might appear as a cord wrapping around each other like a straitjacket to keep the other person locked in. If you obsess over another person, this is what the cords look like.

Love is more permissive than this. It doesn't seek to lock the other person in and keep them bound to you, but simply stays as a heart connection. This enables each of you to live your own life and be your own person while feeling loved and supported by that love.

THE DIFFERENCE BETWEEN SEX AND LOVE

It is also important not to confuse sex and love. The reason that many spiritual traditions have rules about sexual conduct is because of the over-bonding that can result through sex. Cords are attached between the two of you, but if these are not heart cords, they can drain you energetically. The more sexual connections you have that are not love connections, the more you are putting out energy that doesn't bring back love into yourself. It is important to clear non-loving connections of any sort as a way of bringing real love into your life through the Law of Attraction. The Hawaiian forgiveness ritual in Chapter 2 (see pages 52–55) is a very useful way for you to start doing this.

IN ESSENCE

Love attracts love. We are all meant to be loved. We are all lovable. What stops us attracting love is not recognizing this. Attracting love from other people starts with self-love. There may be many reasons you don't recognize that you are worthy of this love. Many of us are damaged by other people's words or actions in childhood or later in life. However, you have the power to look at yourself with fresh eyes at any time of your life and see the real you free from any false ideas you may have adopted about yourself. You can find love in yourself and, when you do so, you can begin to receive love from others. Love is a habit. Love comes out of both thought and action. You can connect with love any time by being gentler with yourself, by being more compassionate with yourself and by being kind to others. Most of all, make a decision today. Decide, whether you fully believe it right now or not, to recognize that you are perfect. Be as kind to yourself as you would be to a small baby. Find in yourself that deep love for the unique you. You will start to notice how you are rewarded as you begin these new loving habits. Not only will you feel better about yourself and your life, but other people will begin to behave differently to you as well.

MY NOTES

CHAPTER 4

Decide your future

'NOTHING IS MORE POWERFUL THAN HABIT.'
OVID

What kind of future do you want? It is time to decide so that you can create your future intentionally rather than by default. Think about what a life of love will look and feel like. The clearer you become about what you want to create, the happier you will be with the results.

In this chapter you will learn how to:

♥ Decide what you want and create an intention to have it

♥ Create a 'love treasure map' so that you can begin to dream about your new life

♥ Create your personal 'love list' through which you can attract new types of relationship, which will help you keep your sense of self

♥ Use your emotions to guide you to keep on track

CASE STUDY: PHILIPPE PETIT

One day in August 1974, something extraordinary happened. The people of New York's Lower Manhattan were going about their ordinary business. There was nothing to indicate that it was a special day, but hundreds of feet above their heads, a man was walking on a cable between the Twin Towers of the World Trade Center.

The man who made this amazing tightrope walk was Philippe Petit, who had begun life as a Parisian street artist. His story is told in the documentary film *Man on Wire* by James Marsh. Philippe was just 18 when he read an article in his dentist's waiting room about the towers, which had not even been built at that point. Nevertheless, he made up his mind that when the towers were built he would walk a high wire between them.

In order to do this walk, he would not only have to have enormous passion and tenacity, but also be incredibly resourceful. Petit planned for six years. He and his friends made several trips to the towers to collect information, then broke into the towers, hid themselves and their equipment over 100 floors up and rigged a steel cable across the huge 43-m (140-ft) divide. That was all before Petit walked across the wire, buffeted by the winds swaying the cable.

On 7 August, in the early morning, Petit stepped out on to the wire. He walked above Manhattan for 45 minutes, back and forth across the cable. He even lay down for a while. He eventually stopped when the police arrived. They arrested him, but Petit had achieved what he had set out to do all those years before. His incredible feat made headlines all over the world.

What makes this such an inspiring story for me is the fact that Petit believed in his vision so much that he was able to keep his faith and keep going, despite many difficulties and obstacles along the way.

Whatever *you* want to create in your life you can do it, too, if you know what you want and why. You can hold the picture of what you want in your mind and focus on it, no matter what the odds.

Create a vision for your future

The Twin Towers weren't even built when Philippe Petit (see case study opposite) first committed to his goal to walk a high wire between them, yet he kept an absolute unwavering belief in his ability to bring about this immense achievement in his life. No one told him he could do this. The belief came from inside him. Do you want your loving future as much as Petit wanted to walk between the Twin Towers? Do you have a picture of what you want to create in your life?

Allow yourself permission to dream about how your future could be. It is not enough just to tell the universe that you want to have love in your life. You need to actively imagine what this will look and feel like when you have it. The spiritual universe responds to the picture of what you want and does its best to bring it towards you as you take real actions to make it happen at the same time. Manifestation comes about as a result of co-creation between you and the spiritual universe.

Treasure maps

When you want to bring something new into your life, it is really useful to create physical images of what you want to manifest. When you see an image every day it reminds you to focus on what you want. It stimulates and feeds your unconscious in a very easy, light way with pictures of your dreams, helping you to create the energy that magnetizes your new happy future towards you.

The idea of treasure maps came originally from the author Shakti Gawain in the 1970s and her writings on creative visualization. Some people now refer to treasure maps as vision boards, visual prayers or universe wish lists. A treasure map is a collection of personally inspiring images, which together form a picture of what your future will be like when your goals are fully realized. Having that treasure map up on your wall will help to draw in the life represented by those images. Your unconscious just loves visual images that provoke an emotional response.

Create your love treasure map

♥ Get hold of a pinboard or a large piece of card and start to collect images that represent your new future. In this case you are going to devote your treasure map to images of a new *loving* future. Just beginning the process of collecting these images can be really motivational and illuminating.

♥ Start looking for happy pictures. Look through magazines and on the internet, find postcards and photos that represent your dreamed new reality. You are looking for any image that will inspire or motivate you to create this new future and bring it to life.

♥ When you have chosen your images, get your glue and scissors and make a collage on your board – just like you did at primary school, but this time with more purpose. The rule of thumb is to do it with joy and abundance. What you feed in energetically to your picture is going to make an impact.

♥ You can also draw the images yourself if that adds even more meaning to your love treasure map. It doesn't matter if you aren't Rembrandt. If a childlike drawing of a house with a family in front of it and a bright-yellow sun in the sky brings you great feelings of happiness, it might be more effective than a perfect photograph from a magazine. The Law of Attraction works on the feelings you attach to an image. The more you can believe that your future is possible and probable, the more of it will be attracted to you.

THE IMAGES TO INCLUDE

Make sure you include images on your love treasure map that reflect the sort of person you will be when you *have* attracted love. Think about what your life will be like *after* you have already achieved this desired future. This will make your unconscious see your future goals not as something you want, but as something that is a foregone conclusion. As soon as this happens, the Law of Attraction can start working its magic and begin to make these pictures a reality.

Perhaps you want pictures of happy friends and family gatherings or of couples holding hands. Think about the life experiences you will have with friends and your loving partner when you have attracted this new life to you. Perhaps you want pictures of a couple travelling together, or having a child together, or a loving couple growing old together? Or a couple getting married, if that's what you want.

Be expansive in your thinking. Remember this is the blueprint that the Law of Attraction will use for your future.

Create a well-rounded life. You could just stick up pictures of people who look like your ideal man/woman, but then what are you going to do with this person when they arrive in your life? What sort of life do you want to have with them? How do you want to be treated by them? What kind of life values will you share?

Personally I always make sure I have happy scenes of activities I want to pull into my life to create a light, happy, rich life with my friends and partner. You might want to have pictures of dancing, being with animals, spending times in a beautiful place. One picture I have always liked on my treasure map is an image I found in a travel magazine of a couple climbing up a hiking trail together. They look happy, fit, loving and healthy and they are in a beautiful place. I create a future with travel, love and well being all in one hit!

You'll find you get quite choosy when you start collecting your pictures. You may start with a big pile of pictures and, the more you look at them and get a feel for them, the more you will start to discriminate between those that really resonate with you and those that are just 'so-so'. The guideline? When in doubt chuck them out. Choose only images that are truly nurturing for your soul. Colour is good; black and white isn't as stimulating to the unconscious as colour. Create a big, bold, bright dream future through your images if you want to create a big, bold future in your reality.

THE FINISHED MAP

Where are you going to put your treasure map? I put mine somewhere
I can catch sight of it every day on a wall near where I work. But you could
also choose to place it near your love altar (see page 131), in the bedroom as
a reminder to bring love in each morning or even in the corner of your house
associated with love from a feng shui point of view. You can even carry a
mini collage in your purse or in the front of a notebook you use regularly.

This is a dynamic process. You don't have to keep the images you started with
just because they are stuck on the board. Get rid of any picture as soon as it stops
inspiring you. Change your pictures, update them. Take delight in your treasure
map each day. It was the author William W. Purkey who first said: 'You've gotta
dance like there's nobody watching... Sing like there's nobody listening' and it is
a great sentiment. I want your pictures to dance and sing so that they dance and
sing to your soul and that vibration goes out to the universe and attracts in love
from everywhere.

In summary:

i) *Make your future visual: use pictures not words.*

ii) *Choose images that are meaningful to you and make you feel good.*

iii) *Keep it private so that you aren't influenced by other people's ideas about what's
right for you.*

By the way, the results can be immediate. I put a picture of a holiday I wanted
to create on my life treasure map and manifested it that very day when a friend
invited me away!

Your love list

Spend as long as you like thinking about what you want to create in your life. As well as your love treasure map, keep an ongoing love list of what you want in the love area of your life. A love list is your definition of what love is for you.

WHAT DO YOU WANT?

A love list starts by clarifying what you want in your life.

What do you really enjoy doing with your life? What kind of activities will give you the feeling of having love in your life? What kind of relationships would you have? What kind of people would be present?

Write down what your life will be like when it is full of love. Imagine and describe in words every area of your life, not just romantic relationships. How will your life change when you have become this new loving person who finds it so easy to attract love? Picasso said: 'Every child is an artist. The problem is how to remain an artist after he grows up.' Be imaginative. Be creative. Indulge yourself. Write down what you really want. Make sure that you don't in any way write down what you think other people would want you to have. Censorship kills dreams. Be as imaginative as you were as a child.

Once you start writing you'll find that you can write really expansively. Check your feelings as you go along. If there is even a tiny part of you that says I am not sure I want this bit, then cut it out and start again.

Remember that when we do something for the very first time it doesn't necessarily feel totally easy or natural because, of course, it is the very first time. Once you have let yourself get into the swing of this new habit of thinking about a happy, loving future it will become natural. You'll soon discover all these wonderful dreams you have for the future. Let your mind wander naturally. Explore each picture in turn. Make little adjustments and alterations.

It is important to play, not work at this. Personally I find I do this best by jotting down ideas in a special book I have bought for my love list. Then I can decant the best ideas on to a wall chart so that I have them near me at all times.

Don't force yourself. You will be most creative when you are comfortable, lying in the sun or in a hot bath, meditating or as you wake up in the morning. Just relax and let the ideas come naturally.

CASE STUDY: CLAIRE'S LOVE LIST

Here's the love list that one of my clients, Claire, came up with:

For me having a life full of love means:

♥ Having a committed relationship with a man who loves me and whom I love equally. We live together and enjoy each other's company every day.

♥ We are married because that symbolizes the deep commitment we have made together and because we want to tell the world that we value each other so much.

♥ I wake up with my husband in the morning and go to sleep with him at night.

♥ We have a family together and as a family we share a deep bond, which means we talk about things together, we share joyful experiences and we laugh every day. We eat together at least once a day and always make time every day to talk and relax, and each week to do something interesting together as we recognize that spending time with each other without other interruptions shows us how important we are to each other.

♥ I show my love by being affectionate to my partner. We buy each other big gifts and little gifts even when it isn't a special occasion. We tell each other how special the other person is and look for different ways to please each other. We hold hands and kiss each other and show our love through touch.

♥ We have a great sex life!

♥ We make sure we communicate the things that are most important to us so that we build intimacy and trust more and more every day.

♥ I am surrounded by friends whom I love and who love me, which for me means pursuing different interests together, being able to talk freely without judgement and laughing and having fun together. We also give each other space, knowing that we will still be in each other's lives throughout many different experiences. We listen to each other when we need someone to talk to when times are mixed, and share the joy when things are going well. My friends are happy for me to be the best I can be and to have a loving relationship and an abundant, joyous life.

♥ Having love in my life means having children with my husband and building a family life that includes spending time with our relatives and having family gatherings, both to celebrate special events and also just to spend time together when we feel like it. I often have dinners and Sunday lunches, which are joyous occasions where friends and family come to share time together and just chat and have a good time.

♥ I give myself space every day to treat myself well. I look after my mind, body and spirit so that I feel loving to myself. I pamper myself if I have had a busy day and buy myself a gift or take time for a massage so that I lift up my spirits.

♥ I recognize when I meet someone whose energies affect me negatively and I keep my distance from them and say no when I know things aren't right for me. I let go of my own need to create drama and to play the judge or the victim.

♥ I have a mix of older friends and new friends, so that I constantly refresh my life and interests while retaining a feeling of shared love and experiences.

♥ I trust myself and I trust the people in my life so that we can share our lives without judgement.

♥ I make sure I include in my life lots of interests, doing things that I love, including travel, learning about new things and just trying something that I have never tried before to find out whether it contributes to my life. The more fun things I do, the more I appreciate myself and my life.

♥ I go to the gym, and eat healthily so that I love my body and feel good physically.

♥ I create a loving home by getting rid of the things in it which I don't like when I look at them, and I look around every day and love the beauty of the things I own.

♥ I give myself the time to discover things and interests that are personally meaningful to me and create a sense of purpose in my life.

♥ Most importantly I commit to having love around me in a way that keeps my sense of self. I commit to loving myself first, and by loving myself, attract love at all levels of my life.

WHY DO YOU WANT THIS?

Look at what you have written in your love list. Then next to each idea for your future write down some reasons *why* this is so important for you to have in your life. If you decide that it is a 'nice to have' rather than a 'must', then I would suggest that you question whether you really feel passionate enough about it to manifest it in your life. Think about what having this in your life will add to your life. What positive feelings will it bring you? Being clear on *why* you want a *what* will really get the good feelings attached to your future dreams.

Read through your love list. Make it as personal as possible. Then really *feel* that dream coming alive. If you are imagining being with your new love, imagine what your friends will say to you and about you, imagine what loving words you and your partner will exchange. Where will you eat and sleep? What kinds of activities will you do together? What will your life be like on a daily basis? How will you demonstrate your love to each other? Will you travel? Will you write each other love notes? Will you give each other little gifts? What is the most meaningful way someone can demonstrate love to you?

Dream that it is happening and, most importantly, feel it. Remember the more you charge your dreams with emotion and feeling, the more you activate the Law of Attraction.

Harnessing the power of feelings

One thing people don't always understand about the Law of Attraction is that it works on *feeling*. A client says something like: 'Well, I wrote out my goals, but nothing happened.' So I ask: 'What do you feel when you imagine achieving your goals?'

I might get an answer like 'not much' or 'I really want these things to happen in my life, but I don't know how to make them happen.'

If I probe a little more, they might say something like: 'I don't *feel* I can really make that sort of thing happen to me.'

The key word here is 'feel'. If you *think* you want one kind of life, but *feel* you will get or deserve another kind, guess which the Law of Attraction will bring you? The Law of Attraction is magnetic. Emotion carries a higher charge of energy than logical, conscious thought.

Every time you think about your past or your future you have an emotion attached to the image in your mind. To demonstrate this, think about the following questions:

Do you remember what freshly cooked bread tastes like?

How about the smell of freshly laundered sheets?

Remember a time when you felt really good about something or someone?

Do you have a memory of a favourite piece of music?

Recalling pictures or smells or tastes brings up feelings. Although those memories happened in the past, the feelings attached can be brought into the present.

You can make the future happen by putting memories into the future, too. By visualizing what you want in lots of detail, imagining what it will feel like when you are living that future dream, your unconscious starts to believe that it is real. The energy of this future 'memory' acts as a magnet, pulling your new future into your life. The trick is making sure you feel joyful. The stronger your feelings, the easier you will find it to attract what you want.

This is also why it is so vital to spend time on your feelings of loving yourself first before you start creating a new future – otherwise you will just attract what you have always attracted. Negative emotion is a very powerful thing. If you are full of anger you will attract angry people and experiences that bring more anger into your life. If you are full of sadness or unresolved grief from lost love or bad childhood experiences, then you are going to keep creating more loss and sadness in your life through the Law of Attraction. It is therefore enormously important to identify any unresolved negative emotions and to resolve them, as they act as big energy blocks in your unconscious, magnetizing experiences towards you.

Once you have dealt with negative emotions you create an energy gap within your unconscious. Because the highest energy in the universe is love, this will flow into the spaces you have created. Once you feel loved and love yourself, you will attract loving experiences and loving people into your life.

When you think of that new life, what does it feel like? Does it make you feel happy or excited thinking about it? Or do you not have many feelings about it?

If you can't get excited thinking about your future, then you need to change something in the pictures you are making.

Turning your dreams into intentions

If *feeling* is the first key to success with the Law of Attraction, the second key to success is to make a decision that you will make these dreams happen. As soon as you have made this decision you can turn your 'wants' to 'whens' by creating a series of intentions or goal statements.

CREATING A CLEAR INTENTION

Imagine, for example, that one of your intentions is to manifest a relationship by the end of the year. The reason you want this is because you would like to have a partner to enjoy being with at Christmas. Longer term, you want to settle down and have a family. The first actions you intend to take towards this goal are to join a dating agency and also take up a new weekly dance class so that you get out and meet more people.

Write down your intention (also known as a cosmic order). For example:

'My intention is that I will be with my new loving partner this Christmas.'

Now imagine a specific scene on this exact day – a moment in the future that you can 'freeze-frame' in your mind, like a future memory. Describe this in as much detail as possible and, as you do this, make sure that it evokes strong positive feelings in you. For example:

'It is December 25th. I am sitting at the table in my home next to my romantic partner. I am really loving being with this person. I can smell the food on the table and feel his arm around me. I can hear him saying that he loves me. At this moment I am so happy. I feel so loved. I feel so loving. I feel so alive...'

Describe what you can see, feel and hear in the scene as specifically as possible. Then say to yourself:

'Thank you for this already having happened in the best way for me to create a happy, balanced life, for everyone around me and to the highest good of all concerned.'

Make as many intention statements as you need to fully flesh out your vision of your future.

Follow these rules to create intention statements

♥ Take pen and paper and *write down your intention* (this ensures that you commit to it).

♥ Write your intention in the present tense as if it is happening to you *right now*. (This way you feel your intention becoming real.) *See* it, *feel* it, *hear* it. Create an emotional connection to it.

♥ Be specific about *what* you want.

♥ Be clear *why* you want this – your intention must be personally compelling for it to have sufficient energetic 'charge' to manifest.

♥ Be clear *when* you want this. (This helps you to focus clearly on what you will create.)

♥ Be clear that having this in your life will be *good for you* and everyone else who might be impacted by it.

♥ Decide what you are going to *do* to make this happen as a first step (even if the universe may eventually give it to you in another way).

Now play your part

It's not enough just to think about what you want. The inner work always comes first, but you do need to take some action in the real world as well to manifest your future.

Once you've done the work on the inside, cement your belief that it is going to happen by doing some work on the outside as well. It doesn't really matter what that action is, as long as in your mind it is taking you towards what you want. As the saying goes, 'The Gods help those who help themselves'. Simply look at your dream and decide a first step to getting it.

Look back at your intention statement. Now write down any step you could take towards this. This shows the universe you have committed to this vision. For example:

'I will commit to this new future by joining a dating agency this month and starting salsa classes in September [describe what you will do as specifically as possible]. This is the service and energy that I offer to the universe in return for manifesting my new future.'

THE GODS HELP THOSE WHO HELP THEMSELVES...

If you want to get rich and win the lottery, you have to buy a lottery ticket. If you want to get a great job, then start applying for some. If you want to meet someone, start getting out there – take up some new hobbies, join a dating agency. It doesn't really matter what you do as long as your intention is to make things happen.

When you manifest your dreams they may come about in indirect ways and not seem on the surface at least to have come as a direct consequence of the action you have taken. But it is because you have taken an action that they manifest.

DO I NEED TO KNOW EVERY STEP?

Let's clear up an issue that people are often confused about. Taking action does not mean that you need to know every step that will be required to achieve your dream. It is much more important to be really, really clear about *what* you want, rather than *how* you think you are going to get it. As long as you put energy into your dream in some way, *and keep focusing on what you want*, you will get results. The universe makes miracles happen.

TRUST THE UNIVERSE

OK, having said all this, here's the part where some people start getting doubts. Manifestation takes trust. You need to *trust* and let go of *how* the universe will help you.

Many people who have written to me about their successes and blocks with the Law of Attraction get as far as being clear on what they want and then start doubting. They go back to negative thinking and doubt that they really can achieve their dreams. They don't trust that the power of the universe will sort things out.

What do you do if you are one of these people?

Stay calm. Go back to Chapters 1 and 2 and consider the following: are you clinging on to some of your old thought patterns? Have you forgiven yourself and others for your past hurts?

Don't try to deny negative or questioning thoughts or batter them down.

AVOID MOLE-BASHING

When I catch people trying to suppress what they are really thinking, it reminds me of the Japanese game called *Moguratati* (mole-bashing), which I used to play in games arcades when I lived in Tokyo. There is a board in front of you with lots of holes in it. As an alarm sounds, a mole pops its head out of a hole and you have to bash it down again. You don't know where the mole is going to come up, so you have to keep alert at all times. Then more than one mole sticks its head up. The game gets faster and faster, with more and more moles appearing.

I regard negative thoughts as a bit like moles. If you just hit them on the head they are only going to stick their heads up somewhere else. They aren't going to go away by you pretending they aren't there.

So, stop bashing your thoughts. Just softly observe them. Acknowledge that these thoughts have appeared for a reason. They are just telling you that they are there so that you have the chance to let go of them once and for all.

Once you have acknowledged them, then gently question them. Here are a few questions to get started with:

Is this a useful way for me to think if I want to attract more love into my life?

Is this a useful way to think if I want to attract all *the love I intend to have in my life?*

Is this a useful way to think if I am going to attract every single one of my dreams in the way I have written them down on my love list?

Is this a useful way to think if I am going to attract every single one of my dreams in the way I have put them on my love treasure map?

What would be a more trusting way of thinking?

What would be a more abundant way of thinking?

What would be a happier way of thinking?

What way of thinking would help me to achieve what I want?

What resources do I already have to achieve what I want?

What other beliefs would it be useful to adopt to attract the life I want?

What evidence can I find now to support these beliefs in my life?

Above all, be gentle with yourself. Just keep focusing back on what you want, imagining your new life as if it is happening to you right now. The more you fill out that life in your head, the easier it will be to begin to trust it will happen.

Why 'not wanting something' brings it to you

Here's another trap many of us fall into. Instead of spending our time thinking about how to create a particular future that we do want, we spend our time thinking about how we are going to avoid all those things we don't want.

If you are not feeling particularly happy or if you have a chequered history with love, then it's an easy trap to fall into. How many times do you catch yourself having the 'don't want' thoughts?

Here is a common one: 'My goal is to make sure I am never alone or single again.'

When you create a negative intention like this, the universe gets a picture from you of a poor, unhappy person and probably gets a burst of strong emotion attached to it as well. The image and thought forms are so strong that the universe receives the image loud and clear. Being a perfectly responsive universe, it does its best to create the intention it has seen and felt for you. The result is that you inadvertently attract more 'being unhappy and lonely' experiences towards you.

When you catch yourself doing a 'don't want', think about how you could turn it into a 'want' statement instead. For example, 'I want to be with a romantic partner by XX date' or 'My goal is to make sure I see friends for dinner twice a week.'

Manifestation boosters

Changing your beliefs is a way of boosting your magnetic power so that you attract love into your life easily. When you change your thoughts, you change your energy vibration. The more positive your vibration, the easier you are going to find it to attract your dreams and make them into your new reality.

There are various other ways you can boost your magnetic power as well. Here are two more that have proved very successful: the laughter method and the 'acting as though something is true' tactic.

LAUGHTER METHOD

This is one of the simplest things you could ever do. The spiritual universe is a very light, happy vibration. When you manifest happiness, you link into the spiritual universe through your thoughts. If you can be light and happy as you think about what you want to magnetize towards you, then you are going to be very successful. All you have to do is be happy. About 30 minutes of concentrated happiness is enough to raise your vibration to the right level.

I would suggest:

♥ Watching a good laugh-out-loud comedy on TV or on DVD

♥ Dancing around to some stupid music

♥ Playing a silly game with children or as if you were still a child

As soon as you have finished, imagine your future as though it is happening to you right now.

ACT AS THOUGH...

If you act as if something is true, then it often becomes true. Act as though you are lovable and you will find people pick up on the difference in your behaviour. You give off different vibes. Your body language changes. You look happier. You really feel happier. And guess what? People want to be around you more. You are more fun to be around. The end result is you get more love in your life. Then, because you are getting more love in your life, you feel more lovable. You give it out and receive it back. It is a self-nurturing cycle.

Now you may feel first of all that you are acting, but the more you do something, the more it becomes a habit and soon it becomes totally unconscious behaviour. Before too long it doesn't feel like acting at all. In fact itjust becomes part of your identity.

Say thank you

Finally, remember to say thank you in advance to the universe for what it is about to bring into your life. We always say thank you because, in one part of the universe, this change has already been created. Expressing gratitude in advance shows the universe that your beliefs are fully trusting in your ability to manifest this change.

Then keep a look out. As long as you keep taking action and focus on what you want, the universe will bring you what you need in order to keep you on the right path.

IN ESSENCE

What is your vision of your future? How often do you sit down and really think about the kind of life you want to build? We are co-creators of our futures. If you put in the effort and focus, then the universe will help you by bringing you people and opportunities to change your life. Being a co-creator gives you power and responsibility. You can bring more of what you want into your life and at the same time have less of what you don't want. It all begins with forming a clear, fresh vision of your future.

Take the time to really think about the loving life you want now. Keep your eye on *what* you want rather than the *how* you are going to get it. Just let go of the *how* for the time being. The universe will sort that out for you in good time. The clearer you can be with your vision, the better. How clear are the pictures you have of this life? Can you gather pictures to help you visualize? Bright, colourful pictures are attractive and memorable for the mind.

To help you to refine your vision, ask yourself *why* you really want this future. Then chuck out anything you don't feel strongly about. Use your emotions as a guide to keep you on track so that you ask for what you truly want.

Forming a clear vision is the first step forward towards what you want. Then you can begin to take actions, one at a time, to create your vision. You still don't need to be able to see the whole path to the end goal, but actions show the universe that you are committed to creating this new life. With each action, keep focusing on what you want and trust that the universe knows how best to help you to bring about this happy, loving future.

MY NOTES

CHAPTER 5

Dream your future

'ALL THAT WE SEE OR SEEM IS BUT A DREAM
WITHIN A DREAM.'

EDGAR ALLAN POE

Once you have had a taste of loving yourself and being loved by another person you will never want to go back into lack again. Attracting love isn't something you do once and then forget about. It is about a changed way of living in the world. New daily habits can help you to continue your 'love state', as can night-time dreaming.

The Law of Attraction doesn't stop working just because you are asleep. Indeed in many spiritual traditions this is the best time to attract a new life as you can bypass your conscious mind and contact your spiritual helpers, who will help you to change your life forever.

In this chapter you will learn how to:

♥ Work with your dreams to explore where you are in your life

♥ Make a dream catcher

♥ Use daytime dreaming to reinforce your link with the spiritual universe

♥ Meditate

Dream life

Edgar Allan Poe's quotation about seeing a dream within a dream is also the view of many spiritual traditions across the planet. They see everyday life as a form of dream. When you are asleep you are still living your life within the spiritual universe, as it is just the conscious part of you that is asleep. In the physical universe, life is bound by the laws of time and space and matter. In other vibrations of the universe there is no time or space; no now, and no past, present or future. There is only what we call 'internal reality' – the 'you' who is not contained in a physical body.

If life is just a different dream, then isn't it logical that dreams are just a different part of your life? Dreams are what link us to the invisible spiritual universe: the connecting channel, if you will, between this world and the world we can't see but where our non-physical bodies reside. You can actively work with your dreams as a way of helping you to heal blocks and to activate and enhance your love attraction.

SLEEP

In ancient spiritual traditions sleep is seen as the basic state out of which we all come. Before we are born into a physical body on this earth we are naturally in a sleep state, without eyes, ears, nose, tongue and touch. In sleep we return once more to this place we came from, to connect again with the invisible world of the spiritual universe.

You sleep for about one-third of your life. For the average person that's over 25 years of your life spent in a non-waking state. Not all of your time asleep is spent dreaming, but researchers reckon that at least ten years of your life is spent inside a sleeping dream.

Working with your dreams

All of us dream. Some of us appear to dream more than others only because we are better at remembering our dreams. If you are not someone who regularly remembers their dreams, don't worry. It is something you can train yourself to do with practice.

Dreams work on two levels. In broad terms the two types of dreams are:

i) *Objective dreams – a psychic dream about a real event*

ii) *Subjective dreams – personal dreams that can give insights into your current thinking and development*

Dreams show us, in either symbols or images, what we are focusing on. Dreams talk to us in pictures and images because a picture is a much stronger representation of an idea than a word can ever be. Sometimes the image is very obvious and easy to interpret. Sometimes it doesn't make sense at first.

At the same time dreams provide a direct channel for the spiritual universe to communicate with us. At night, as you sleep, it is as if there is a direct telephone line opened up between your unconscious self and your higher self and the whole invisible universe, without the block of your conscious mind getting in the way. If you are naturally psychic you may receive future knowledge through dreams or trance about events that are going to happen as you access what are called the Akashic records. This is the infinite store of knowledge, like a library, within the spiritual universe where everything about *you* – your past, present and future – is held.

Your spirit knows that the universe is one of infinite possibilities. Every resource that you will ever need to resolve any issue is available to you. It works with your unconscious at night to bring this to your attention. Dreams help you to recognize misconceptions you hold about yourself, different facets of yourself along with your fears, hopes and all other emotions.

CREATIVE DREAMING

Creative or lucid dreaming is a way of working with your dreams to explore where you are in your life and to reach out to the wisdom of your guides and your higher self. Shamans practise this type of dreaming, which means dreaming in an intentional way, keeping control of the outcome of the dream. Lucid dreaming is the more commonly used term, but I like 'creative dreaming' because it emphasizes that you can control dreaming and use it creatively at will. In a lucid dream you are aware that you are dreaming even as you experience the dream. As you wake within the dream you can then direct the dream to wherever you want to take it.

You can learn this same skill as a way to work with your dreams for self-knowledge and for clearing negative emotions as you progress along your love-attraction journey.

The Law of Attraction and dreams

The Law of Attraction helps you attract into your life what you are focusing on at all levels of your being, whether you are awake or asleep. As soon as you begin to work with your dreams to attract love, you will be given insights into what is going on in your life, intuition about people you meet and events you experience as well as anything that still needs to be healed or resolved.

By working with your dreams, you will get clues as to what is going on in your unconscious thinking and be able to resolve issues at the deepest levels. At the same time this will help you to practise daily at communicating with your higher self to bring in love every day.

Dreams are sources of great wisdom. By becoming aware of your dream travels each night, you can tap into higher guidance for your waking state every day.

There are two ways to help attract love through dreaming – dream interpreting and the RISC technique.

METHOD 1: DREAM INTERPRETING

This method uses dreams as a spyhole on to your inner world. Deliberately remembering your dream gives you clues as to what stage you have reached in moving on from past hurts or patterns of attracting love. Dreams can alert you to specific issues that need to be dealt with before you can move on to the next stage. They let you know both the problem and often the solution as well. Dreams will weave a story out of your everyday experiences and imagination to bring the issue to your attention.

An easy way to begin working with your dreams is to *pay attention*. One of my spiritual teachers used to tell me: 'If you don't pay attention, you'll pay in other ways' (meaning pain and suffering, I think!). You can also put it another way – pay attention and you'll get a big, positive pay-off as well. As soon as you start to pay attention to your dreams the spiritual universe will then help you by giving you dream messages about how you can overcome the issue and move on with your life.

There are many books on the subject of dream symbol interpretations. Some symbols can be intensely personal in their meanings. Other symbols are 'archetypes'

and have universal meanings. For example, if you dream about a house, this is generally taken to be the 'self'. You can look up these universal meanings in dream books, but do be aware that some symbols will also have unique meanings for you. A particular person in a dream represents a part of your personality that you may or may not be aware of. If there is a dominant character in the dream it is useful to think about the characteristics of that person. How do they mirror aspects of yourself? If you are not certain, it may be because he or she is mirroring something that you are unaware of in yourself. If you are not sure, let the question stay with you until your unconscious gives you some other clues.

It is helpful to spend time thinking about each part of the dream in turn. What does each event or image mean to you? Some dreams point to our fears and some to our desires. What idea do you most associate with the particular image? For example, I associate water with the flow of emotions, so a leaky tap for me is emotions leaking out when I am trying to suppress them. A baby for me symbolizes the part of me that is undeveloped and needs protecting. A fast car is a method of getting somewhere. As well as symbolizing learning, a school symbolizes a place where there are rules and restrictions, but also perhaps safety and security.

Let your personal association with each image come into your mind and, if you are not certain, ask for another dream to clarify whatever you are still not sure about.

Set intentions to dream

♥ Keep a pad of paper and a pen by your bedside at night. Intend before you go to sleep that you will dream about whatever you want to know about. Here are some examples of the sort of intentions you could set:
'I intend to dream about anything that is blocking me from having a happy relationship right now.'
'I intend to dream about how I can overcome this/these blocks.'
'I intend to dream about what actions would be useful for me to take right now that will move my life forward to love, in a way that is to my highest good.'

♥ Once you have set an intention to dream and remember the relevant parts of the dream, your unconscious will know that you are serious and you are more likely to remember what's important when you wake up in the morning.

♥ As soon as you awaken, write down as much of the dream as possible. Pay attention to the story, the characters, the setting of the dream, the events and most importantly the feeling you were left with. By recognizing this feeling you will often get the meaning intuitively.

METHOD 2: THE RISC TECHNIQUE

As you begin to clear and untangle the old belief habits that have prevented you from attracting love in the past, you may find that you naturally experience vivid dreams. This is a good indicator that you are in the middle of a shift in your life. In your dreams, your higher self and your unconscious will seek to resolve anything that needs resolving. It is good to recognize that, even with a dream that is not entirely comfortable to you, your higher self is showing you what you are ready to resolve.

If you have a dream with negative feelings, you can employ a very effective and now widely used tool developed by Dr Rosalind Cartwright called the RISC Technique. It has four steps to it.

R = Recognize
Notice when you are having a dream that leaves you feeling negative. For example, you may wake up feeling afraid, tearful or stressed.

I = Identify
Think about the characters and story of the dream. What happened that made you feel uncomfortable? What precisely was emotional or disturbing about the dream?

S = Stop
Once you have practised lucid dreaming (see page 106), it becomes very easy to stop a dream the moment it becomes uncomfortable. As soon as you become aware of the negative feelings, either wake yourself up or change the plot within the dream.

C = Change
You can change the storyline within the dream and you can also transform your thinking about your dream after you awaken. One of the simplest ways to break the dream is to physically turn over. We tend to find it easier to lucid dream lying on our right sides. Turn to your left and the plot line will change anyway. When you wake up, you can imagine where you wanted the dream story to go and rehearse the new ending. For example, if you felt weak or helpless during the dream, make yourself strong in your actions. Stand up for yourself. You can change any dream to have an empowering outcome.

Practising this technique stops recurring dreams, but most importantly helps you to resolve deep emotional issues.

Love dream catcher

The dream catcher is a psychic protection tool. Of Native American origin, dream catchers are made to hang above the bed and catch bad dreams like a spider catches its prey inside the web. According to legend, the dream catcher ensures that only good dreams enter your mind when you dream at night. It also protects against general negative energies.

Making your own dream catcher rather than buying one is far more powerful as it becomes like any other psychic tool or ritual – a repository for your intention to let go of the old stuff in your life and replace it with the new.

Your dream catcher then becomes something you can hang over your bed and see last thing at night and first thing in the morning as a symbol of this new you. I have two dream catchers myself – one made especially for me by hand and strewn with little rose-quartz crystals and one that I made myself, which contains various feathers and stones that have particular meanings for me.

Make a love dream catcher

Make this for yourself and it can become another tool to attract love into your life through the power of the Law of Attraction.

Either bend a wire coathanger into a circle or purchase a large metal or wooden ring from a craft shop. This will form the outside of your 'web'.

♥ Take some ribbon or suede lacing and glue one end to the ring, then wrap the ribbon tightly around and around the ring until it is completely covered. Stick the end of the ribbon down with glue to secure it in place.

♥ Now take some stiff thread and tie one end to the ring. You are going to make a web of thread across the ring by making half-hitch knots at evenly spaced intervals around the ring. To do this take the thread, loop it over the ring, then bring it back towards you by pulling it through the space between the thread and the ring. Keeping the thread taut between each knot, work around the ring, spacing your knots evenly – about 2.5 cm (1 in) or 5 cm (2 in) apart.

♥ As you work, you can thread small beads or crystals on to the thread if you like. I suggest clear quartz, turquoise or rose quartz as these are crystals associated with love and protection.

♥ Once you have finished the outer 'row', work an inner 'row' by placing each knot between the knots of the previous row. Continue making inner rows in this way, working towards the middle of the web, until all you are left with is a tiny hole in the centre. Put a feather or shell in this central point and then tie the thread to secure it; and glue if necessary.

♥ To complete the dream catcher, attach feather tassels to what will be the 'bottom' of the ring when it is hung up. String feathers and beads on to a piece of thread or suede and secure these to the ring. To finish, make a suede loop for the top, by which to hang it up.

♥ Now create your intention for the dream catcher. Take some time and sit
with it. Make the decision that it will be a tool to help you remove from your
life forever the unhelpful energetic thought forms that have prevented you
from receiving love in abundance and to your highest good. Intend that it is
an instrument to bring you healing in your dreams so that you are open to
love and receive all the love available in life, with the help of your higher
self and spirit guides.

♥ Now hang the dream catcher above your bed.

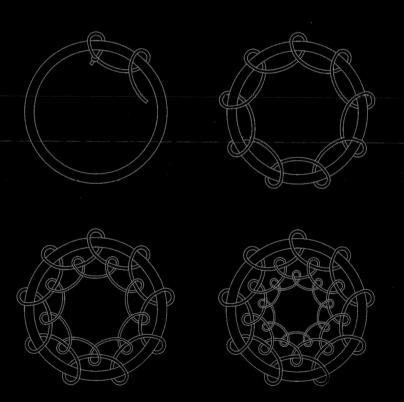

Daytime dreaming

You can take even more control of your love dreams by dreaming during the day as well as at night.

Many spiritual traditions don't just use dreams for answers to life. They also deliberately change one's conscious state to replicate the conditions found in dreaming, thereby accessing the higher levels of the universe beyond the constraints of time and space to find great wisdom and guidance. In ancient cultures such as Babylon, dreams were a way of receiving messages from the gods. Through dreams and changes of conscious state you could foretell the future or understand divine will. In Native American culture shamans alter their states of awareness deliberately to communicate with the subtle energies of spirit animals and guides. Some traditions use natural drugs to produce a trance, others use drumming to produce ecstatic states, some use different forms of meditation.

All of these have the same effect – to take you out of your normal waking state to a place where your brainwaves slow down, just as they do in sleeping, to either alpha-wave level or the even slower theta-wave level.

As this happens, your vibration changes and you open up a clear channel between your conscious mind and your unconscious mind, as well as between your unconscious mind and your higher self and spirit guides. This allows an easier flow of messages between the higher realms of the spiritual universe and the 'you' sitting here in the material world.

MEDITATION AND TRANCE

I have always thought the word meditation slightly off-putting. When I was younger I used to think it was something really difficult that you had to spend years learning how to do. I got that impression partly from all those pictures of Zen monks sitting cross-legged in silence and partly from the exorbitant prices that some institutions charge for meditation classes.

You don't need to be an amazingly trained or evolved person to meditate or go into a trance. When I trained as a hypnotherapist and started experimenting with self-hypnosis I realized I didn't feel much different in that state than I did when sitting looking out over the famous Ryoanji Zen meditation garden in Japan.

There are many different forms of trance. During the day we all slip naturally in and out of different states, which are mild trances. When I am driving, for example, I find I reach my destination and realize that I have been driving without really thinking at all about what I was doing. That's a form of trance. Relaxing deeply while sitting in your favourite chair listening to a beautiful piece of classical music is a form of trance. Daydreaming is trance. That in-between state when you are neither asleep nor fully awake first thing in the morning is a form of trance.

All that 'meditate' means is to 'go to the centre'. When you are meditating your focus changes. You can learn to do this in various ways.

Some people prefer the Eastern form of meditation, where you sit straight-backed on a chair or cross-legged in silence, focusing on only one idea and letting go of other thoughts that drift into your awareness.

Personally, I prefer a more focused trance, called 'active meditation', with a background of sound or music in the shamanistic tradition. In this method, you can either sit or lie down. You can buy guided shamanic healing trances or choose your own piece of gentle classical music to listen to.

When you have learned to relax easily, you can ask to meet your guides to give you messages in your room of relaxation while you are in this trance state. Remember that the messages you receive may well be in the form of symbols or pictures flashing into your mind. When you come out of the meditation let your mind focus softly on what you have received until the meaning of the message comes to your mind.

Learn to meditate

♥ Set yourself a time limit. I would start with about 15 minutes in total and then progress to a regular 30-minute meditation.

♥ Find a place free of any distractions (see page 152) in which to meditate.

♥ Sit straight-backed in a chair. Your legs should be uncrossed. This is the ideal position for meditation as it opens up the energy channel of the spine, which can act as a conductor, bringing down higher vibration energies from the spiritual universe into this world. Close your eyes and take a big deep breath, then let it out through the mouth. Let your body relax. Let your arms rest gently on your lap, let your legs sink into the floor.

♥ Set your intention before you close your eyes. What do you want to learn by meditating today? Or do you just want to see what your unconscious reveals in the trance state? Either is fine. Your unconscious will help you to become aware of the answer to specific questions or will throw up images that will help you generally in your personal progress.

♥ Now take two more deep breaths and exhale through the mouth. As you breathe out, feel any tension just drop out of your body. You can say to yourself: 'As I breathe out, all tensions and worries and stresses of the day melt away into the floor below. I am deeply relaxed.'

♥ Feel your eyelids become heavy. If you wish, you can check your eyelids. Slowly open them and close them, feeling the relief of being able to close them again, and go further into deep relaxation – this wonderful state of daytime dreaming meditation.

♥ Now imagine that there is an elevator in front of you. You walk into the elevator and see that there are ten floors. You are currently on the tenth floor and you can press the button with '1' on it so that you can go all the way down. As the elevator descends, each button lights up in turn so that you can see the numbers flashing down, 10, 9, 8, 7, 6, 5, 4, 3, 2, 1.

♥ When you reach the first floor you will see the door to a room in front of you. This is your room of relaxation. There is a bed here. It looks so comfortable. Enter the room and lie down and totally relax.

♥ Remain in this place for five minutes or so at first (extend the time as you become more practised).

♥ When you want to come out, just get back into the elevator and press the button to the tenth floor. See the numbers going up from one to ten. When you reach the ninth floor, feel the energy beginning to return to your body. As you reach the tenth floor take a big deep breath. Open your eyes and slowly bring yourself up to conscious awareness, feeling the energy return to your legs and arms and eyes and mouth and head and neck. Feel your breathing come back to normal. Wake up easily and when you are ready you can get up.

IN ESSENCE

At night your conscious mind can step out of the way and your powerful link to the spiritual universe is revealed. You are used to dreaming. You may not have ever thought of using your dreams to help you to find love. Start to become aware of the dreams you have at night-time. The spiritual universe sends you messages in your dreams to help you with your personal development and everyday life.

If you want to ask for help around a particular area of your life – find out if you have a block or how to get over a block – you can practise lucid dreaming. Deliberately use dreams creatively to discover more about your progress to love. Meditation is a form of daytime dreaming which also links you to the spiritual universe and provides you with its wisdom. You can interpret the symbols you see in your meditation in the same way as those in your dreams.

Meditation will also help you to become sensitive to other energies within the spiritual universe and will reinforce any of the exercises you do in the next two chapters.

MY NOTES

CHAPTER 6

Love rituals

'THE MIRACLE IS NOT TO FLY IN THE AIR, OR WALK
ON THE WATER, BUT TO WALK ON THE EARTH.'
CHINESE PROVERB

♥

This chapter describes some simple love rituals you can carry out. Spiritual rituals and ceremonies are a way of connecting to the sacred and divine universe. They are used by many spiritual traditions as a way of reinforcing the belief that what you want to manifest will actually happen.

When you carry out a ritual you are acting out symbolically your new, intended future. You show the universe the experience you would like to bring about in your own life by focusing your attention on a symbol of that new life. Performing the ritual in a measured and focused way helps to reinforce the energy of the intention.

In this chapter you will learn how to:

♥ Create a home environment to attract love

♥ Create your own love altar

♥ Use the power of plants, scents and crystals to attract love

Creating a loving home

Your home can become a powerful symbol and living ritual to love. Over the last ten years or so sacred geomancy (a method of divination) and feng shui have become much better known in the West. We now understand what the Chinese and other cultures have known for hundreds of years – that the arrangement of our physical space can impact upon our lives.

I lived in the Far East for a number of years and in one of the offices where I worked one of my wealthiest colleagues had paid her feng shui advisor to look at the layout of the office and advise where she should best place her desk to make money. I remember being quite sceptical at the time, but I gradually learned to take feng shui seriously as she made millions! A turning point for me was when I moved into an apartment and discovered that both my love and wealth corners were missing. Six months after moving in I had resigned my very well-paid job and split up from my boyfriend. A friend who was trained in space-clearing took a look at my home and said it needed urgent work. She spent several hours carrying out energetic clearing in the home. The strangest thing happened immediately afterwards. I came home and found a pool of water in the middle of the floor. An old disconnected pipe in the ceiling, probably over 50 years old, had released the water it was carrying as soon as the energetic clearing had happened. It has often been my experience since that water leaks happen in my home when old stagnant energies are being released. Within a month of the space-clearing I had a new job and a few months later a new relationship.

However much you do or don't want to delve into this subject, I think most of us would at least admit that the space in which we live and work can have a big effect on our mood and general emotions. The home is a powerful mirror of the self.

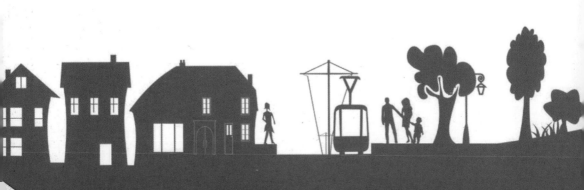

THE ENERGY OF A HOME

When you look around your home, what do you feel? Is it full of things you love to see? Does it lift up your energy when you walk in at night or wake up in the morning, or drag your energy down? Do you feel it is a calm and healing space for you?

A home is an outer representation of what is going on for you inside. You may not be rich enough to have the biggest home or fill it with the most expensive things, but you can still create a loving and nurturing space. This is a very important step towards loving yourself. People who love themselves and attract love create loving environments. Their homes are filled with objects that overflow with loving energy.

You may have had the experience of going into someone's house to feed an animal or water the plants while they are away. Have you ever noticed how even when you walk into an empty house you can still feel the energy or atmosphere connected with the people who live there? It is sometimes so strong that I feel intrusive just by being there. In fact it is a fairly common experience to feel like whispering or walking around quietly in case you disturb something, even if no one is actually there! That's because you unconsciously pick up on energies even if you are unaware of them or haven't been trained in any energy work.

Energy can be even stronger in a home where someone is present. Think about two different situations you may have been exposed to in the past. First, have you ever walked into a home where someone is ill or very depressed? What did you feel? Did you want to hang around or was it an uncomfortable experience? You probably didn't feel entirely at ease because the energy would have been low and would have started to bring down your own energy unless you knew how to protect yourself.

In contrast, have you ever walked into a warm, loving family house where you knew the parents and children were happy and content? I bet you wanted to hang around in that energy. Most of us would because the love energy would be nurturing for anyone who walked in there.

Start to look around your own home and become attuned to the atmosphere. Is it a peaceful place? A happy place? A loving place?

You are in this space regularly, if not every day. If it is not feeding you and reflecting back to you the loving energy that you want in your life, then it's time to change things. It was the designer William Morris who said: 'Have nothing in your house that you do not know to be useful or believe to be beautiful.' I believe we should only own objects that are beautiful or loved. You should feel good when you wake up in the morning and look around. Even if you are not consciously noticing all the things in your home, unconsciously you are doing so.

To make your home ready for your new life, look at everything in there. How would you read your home if you were walking into it for the first time? Remember to pay attention to the garden as well because this is part of your home space.

HAVE A CLEAR-OUT

There are a few very basic things you can do as a way of honouring yourself and your wish to attract new energies and love into your home.

First, start by clearing clutter to get rid of old stagnant energy. It's time to ditch all the useless stuff. Get rid of anything associated with bad times or bad relationships. Get rid, too, of anything associated with a past identity. If you have clothes that make you feel frumpy or unattractive, it doesn't matter how useful they are, chuck them out.

Most of us have too many things. Everything you own is connected to you by an energetic cord connection. How much stuff are you connected to? Think about how much energy that is consuming. If you never have space in your home, how can you have space in your head? We tend to hold on to things because we have a lot vested in them. Sometimes it is about lack. For example, I had better keep that in case I can't afford another one. Let go of your physical bits and pieces and you will find you'll let go of a whole load of mental clutter as well.

PAY ATTENTION TO THE THINGS YOU OWN

Often, someone who is single has pictures of single people on their walls. Instead, and in order to attract love, hang up pictures of happy times with friends and happy couples.

All the material possessions you are carrying around you are part of your past and present identity. Think about what you want to carry forward into the next phase of your life. Do you really need that broken piece of china, or the pair of trousers you liked two years ago, or the vase your aunt gave you as a present? Consider how much freer you will feel with gaps where these things used to be and with space in your life. Imagine what it will be like when you have your new love in your life, or those new friends round for dinner, or your lovely family Christmas in your new happy, loving life. Do you have a table ready for them to eat off? Do you have space in your wardrobe for your new love to hang his or her clothes? Is there room to let people into your home? If there isn't, clear a space.

The rule of the universe is: create a space in your life and the universe will fill it in, so create space with the belief that you will manifest the love you want in the way you want.

CLEAN THE ENERGY OF YOUR HOME

It is important to cleanse the energy of your home from time to time, especially when you have been moving stuff around, by which I mean both material possessions and emotional energy. You should also clean spaces when you move somewhere new or when there has been illness around. Physically clean the room and open windows to let in fresh air. If you have the money and want to do a more dramatic clearing, then paint your home or even re-carpet. The more you do, the more you will change the effects on your life. Make sure your windows are clean, too, as these relate to your eyes, so dirty windows mean you are not seeing clearly. When the room is physically clean, you can clean its energy.

I always clean the energy of a room before I do a major visualization or meditation as well. It is simply a way of raising the vibration of the space and achieving a clear channel through which to magnetize love or whatever you want to manifest towards you.

You don't need to be trained to do space-clearing. We humans are sensory creatures. You can use sound, smell and light to change the vibration of a space. You can also use breath or simply the power of thought. Take a look around your home and think loving thoughts about it. Project love with your mind into every room. This will begin to raise the vibration of your home.

To raise your home's vibration, first of all think about the lighting there. It should feel welcoming and warm. Lighting candles is a lovely way to change the energy of a room.

Music is a very quick way to change the vibration of a space, which is why it is used in every sacred tradition. Every type of music has an effect on vibration. You'll need to experiment, but personally I find classical, especially violin, music to be very effective in space-clearing. Japanese and shamanic drumming can bring a very quick change in vibration if you are going to do a ritual within a room. Pop music can bring in a happy or fun vibration that can be very welcoming, but be careful of any music with negative, unloving lyrics. Remember every thought affects the vibration around you. Fill your home with loving lyrics!

Perform the 'love my home' ritual

Here is an intentional ritual you can do to clear your home as part of your love-attraction strategy.

♥ Start by washing your hands. Take off your shoes and jewellery. Light a white candle and burn some incense.

♥ Now sit quietly for a while and just breathe. Appreciate the space you are in. Notice the energy of your home. Set your thought intention that by cleansing your space today you will bring your new loving life into your home. Be aware of how powerful just this thought is.

♥ You are going to 'smudge' your space, an idea that comes from Native American tradition, using a smudge stick. These are made of dried herbs, commonly sage (burning sage is very powerful), and widely available from mind-body-spirit shops and via the internet. Light a smudge stick to clean old energy out of each room.

♥ Blow out the stick so that smoke comes out of it. Walk around your home and make sure the smoke wafts into every corner clearing out the old energy. As you walk around, state your intention to blow out the old energy and let in the new.

♥ Clap in each corner of each room low down, in the middle and high up to shift the energy. You can also chant a mantra if you know one, for example the Green Tara goddess mantra (see page 152), or just state your intention loudly to the house.

♥ Bells are used traditionally in many places as a way of getting rid of negative spirits. Ring the bell in the centre of the room and in each corner of the room to lift the energy after you have clapped. (If you have one, a traditional musical instrument from Asia called a singing bowl works very well instead of a bell.)

♥ After you have cleaned the energy, wash your hands again. You can now use clean water to anoint the freshly cleansed corners of the rooms. At the same time visualize light coming into the room like a shield all along the outside walls of your home to keep this loving new energy inside. You can also visualize this light as spiralling all around the house.

♥ Finish the ritual by cleansing yourself. Take a bath with sea salt or Epsom salts to disperse any negative energy you have picked up.

BEDROOM

Pay particular attention to the bedroom if you want a new relationship. If you have a bed that is associated with a past love, ideally you want to change the mattress, but if you can't afford to, then smudge all around the bed.

It is also good to have matching bedside tables so that when you and your partner share a bed your power is balanced. In fact, twos of things generally are good in this room.

In Chinese feng shui, red is a good colour to have in the bedroom. Think about putting a red cushion on your bed or perhaps a picture with some red in it.

Plants can raise the energy anywhere in the home and they are great to have in the bedroom. A big plant is better than a small one. You can also experiment with a traditional way to bring romance into the room, which is to keep a vase with red or pink flowers on your bedside table. Make sure the flowers are kept fresh to keep the energy in the room raised. Not all feng shui traditions believe in having plants in the bedroom, by the way, so you may find opinions on this vary.

Creating a love altar

Another powerful ritual you can carry out in your new cleansed space is to set up a love altar. Choose a place where you can create a small sacred space which you can honour and pay attention to on a daily basis. On your altar keep pictures or objects linked with what you want to manifest. You may want to display pictures of you as a happy person, or of couples. Perhaps a symbol associated with a wedding?

Crystals have powerful vibrations, so do place them on your altar. You can put flower offerings (see page 136) or fresh vases of flowers there and burn incense or candles to provide positive energy. You can also offer food or fruit to the energy of the altar.

OPEN UP THE POWER OF YOUR ALTAR

Flow energy each day to your altar by holding your left (receiving) hand up to the universe to receive divine light and your right (giving) hand down to the altar. Clear your mind as you do this and hold only the intention of what you intend to bring into your life.

If you keep an altar it's important to keep it fresh and not let it go stale. If you feel that you can't keep up your altar at any point, then rather than neglect it, take it down consciously with thanks for all it has brought into your life so far. You can burn natural oils to scent your altar, choosing one that is particularly appropriate for you, for example to overcome a fear of loving or of being unloved (see, page 132).

ESSENTIAL OILS FOR YOUR LOVE ALTAR

Property	*Suggested oils*
Overcome fear of loving	Neroli, ylang ylang or carnation
Overcome fear of being unloved	Rose otto
Overcome fear of change	Frankincense, ylang ylang or lavender
Release fear of emotions	Sandalwood, neroli or frankincense
Antidotes to loneliness	Roman camomile or bergamot
Release doubt	Basil, coriander or ylang ylang
Counteract past-abuse thought forms	Rose otto, Roman camomile, mandarin or neroli
Heal the hurt inner child	Neroli, geranium or rose otto
Promote happiness and joy	Rose, orange, jasmine, geranium, clove, ginger or benzoin
Boost self-esteem	Sandalwood, carnation, jasmine, geranium, cedarwood, rose maroc or ylang ylang
Increase self-awareness	Clary sage, pine, bay, mandarin, coriander or jasmine
Connect to divine joy; for burning before meditations for manifesting	Frankincense

Create clay love figures

The more personal your symbols, the more powerful they are. This is an example of a ritual you can do around your altar specifically for a love relationship.

♥ Take clay or moulding clay and make two figures – one to represent you and one your love who will soon manifest in your life. As you make them, intentionally endow them with all the qualities you want to manifest in their lives as they come together. Again, intention is everything. Think about the loving person you are and the loving person you are bringing to you.

♥ When you complete your figures, join them together in some way to symbolize the powerful energetic joining that will soon be happening. You can put the hands together or tie them together loosely with a single red ribbon. The loose binding signifies your intention to bring your love in, with permission from his or her higher self for the higher good of both of you.

♥ Place the figures on your altar and see your love as already manifest in your life.

♥ Remember, always do rituals with the intention that the best outcome for your life as a whole is manifest. Never force anything and certainly never try to force a particular person to come towards you. That is playing with your karma and will not have a good outcome for you.

The power of plants

Flowers and plants look and smell beautiful and have therefore been used in many parts of the world as both love potions and in spiritual ceremonies. Visit a Buddhist temple and you will be overwhelmed by the scent of incense, and also see many vibrantly coloured offerings in the form of fruit and food. In Catholic or Orthodox Christian churches notice how scent is used to raise the energy of the space.

In ancient forms of divination natural fragrant substances like frankincense are used to prepare the diviner to enter a trance so they can access the higher levels of the universe and draw on the wisdom of their spiritual helpers. In Indian tantrism, too, smells are used as a preparation for ritual.

In Chinese tradition, the energy, or *qi* (*ch'i*) of a plant and of the place where something is grown can vary. By choosing particular plants or by choosing a plant from a beautiful location, you can help your own energy. At the most basic level, think how your mood is lifted when you are surrounded by flowers or when you are sitting by a beautiful river. This is because of the energy from the flowers or place. This principle can be used for healing.

The power of the energy of place or nature can be demonstrated in a non-spiritual way. If you sit outdoors in a beautiful green space, scientists know that your cortisol and stress levels are likely to fall as the sights and smells and energy of the space affect you. Similarly, recent studies show that having flowers on the breakfast table to greet you in the morning makes you feel happier for the rest of the day.

In spiritual traditions the effect is more than just stress relief. The *qi* (*ch'i*) of the beauty and scent of nature can be drawn on as a way of attracting love into our lives. Love is a beautiful, joyful, light vibration. To attract it, feed your visual and olfactory senses with beauty and joy and you will attract more love into your life.

THE PUSANGA

Pusangas come from the Peruvian spiritual tradition. They are scented flower potions, which are used as tools to attract whatever you want into your life and are often used as love magic.

In the Amazon, *pusangas* are made from the highest qi (ch'i) plants and from water gathered from sacred or magical places. Plants are chosen for their flowers, shapes, scents and colour and laid out together. Scented liquids are often added to make them highly fragrant. When the *pusangas* is ready it is empowered by the shaman. He blows the intention, for example 'health, wealth and love', into the *pusangas*, sometimes simply using his breath and sometimes using tobacco smoke, which is seen as sacred.

If you wish to make a *pusangas*, you can follow the same principles (see page 137). First gather up some beautiful flowers. You don't need to pick the whole stem, just the flower heads will be enough. It is better to pick your own flowers though, so you can choose that they come from a place of significance.

Certain flowers carry specific meanings in many spiritual traditions (see page 136). They may also carry personal meanings for you. If you can, choose ones that have some relationship to what you want to manifest. If roses mean love to you, for example, include roses. Pay attention to the colours of the flowers and their scents. Again, colour is a very powerful vibration. Thank the flowers as you pick them for the energy they are bringing to you.

FLOWERS AND THEIR MEANINGS

Begonia	Bringing balance into your life
Bougainvillea	Emotional protection and surrender to trust the higher power
Chinese lavender	Transformation
Gardenia	A mirror that doesn't deceive or distort
Hibiscus	Happiness and quiet power
Lily	Purity
Lotus	The divine
Marigold	Readiness for change
Mignonette	Making life beautiful
Myrtle	Overcoming everyday difficulties
Narcissus	Bringing together beauty and the divine
Nasturtium	Encouragement in difficult times
Pink gladioli	Opening up your emotions so you are willing to receive good things in your life
Poinsettia or Christmas flower	Surrendering the ego and being open
Rose	Open heart
Snapdragon	Increasing your power to manifest
Ylang ylang	Clearing your mind of illusion

Create a pusanga

♥ First, cleanse your space using incense or aromatherapy oils to create a beautiful environment.

♥ Lay a cloth out on the floor and arrange your flowers or plants to look beautiful. You could lay them out in a pattern to look like a Buddhist mandala (a sacred circular design that symbolizes the universe).

♥ Add other pretty objects at this point if you like. Glitter or fake jewels are all pretty, so will produce good energy.

♥ Scent the *pusanga* with aromatherapy oils or a natural scent like orange flower water.

♥ Now set your intention. Breathe into the *pusanga* your clear intention to manifest a new sparkling future, as beautiful as the *pusanga* in front of you.

♥ To use the *pusanga* as a scent, add spring water to it and bottle it. Use the liquid to anoint or scent your wrists and neck with your manifestation intention. You might also wish to lay it on your love altar (see page 131), or you could take your *pusanga* to a place that is special to you and leave it as an offering.

GIVE BACK TO THE EARTH TO RECEIVE LOVE

You might like to make an offering of your *pusanga* in a special place. In Peruvian shamanism, offerings, or *offerenda* in Spanish, are given to the earth as a thank you for bringing in positive things into one's life. In the past I have made offerings like this to a very old tree, which carries the energy of hundreds of years of natural wisdom. In ancient wisdom certain places in nature carry a higher energetic charge – the Chinese would call it a higher vibration of *qi* (*ch'i*). By connecting with these places we can take on this energy and raise our own vibrations and our ability to manifest. Why not find your own special place in nature which carries a positive charge for you and make regular offerings there? By doing so you will raise the energy connected with your intention still further. Each time you connect with this place in thought or meditation you then connect with a strong spiritual vibration and raise your own energy, helping you to attract all that you want into your life.

Using crystal power to attract love

A crystal is an object with a specific vibration that acts as a powerful transmitter of energy to and from the universe. Crystals have been used for many years for healing and magical work.

You can also use crystals for love-attraction programming. I suggest that you use either a clear quartz or rose quartz. The rose quartz is the classic crystal of the heart and healing. Simply wearing a rose-quartz necklace or ring, or having it in your home or by your bedside, helps to bring in the vibration of love because that is the vibration the crystal is most tuned into.

To programme the crystal, all you need to do is direct your focus to the crystal. As in every ritual you carry out, your intention is key. Decide what you want to manifest and get a clear picture of it in your mind.

CLEANING YOUR CRYSTAL

First, make sure you have a clean crystal – I mean energetically clean, of course. Don't assume that because you have bought a new crystal from a shop that its energy is clean. When I walk around a crystal shop and hold many of the crystals, I am amazed at the murkiness of the energy of so many of them. It's because they have absorbed the energy of either the location or all the people handling them. Think how you feel after your daily commute and you will understand why your poor crystal needs cleaning. You can leave the crystal outside in the sun and moonlight, partly buried in earth but with the tip sticking out, for three days to clean it. You can also wash the crystal in water and rock salt and, as you do this, imagine the top of your head opening up as you channel universal white light and love down into the crystal, taking away any negative energy.

If you are sensitive you will feel the difference in the energy after cleaning it when you hold it on the palm of your hand. I personally have always felt this as a tingling feeling. Other people feel warmth or cold or just have a sensation of lightness. You will become more attuned to different energies the more you use crystals. Of course if you instinctively don't like the look or feel of a crystal, don't use it. There will be one that is right for you and you should always honour and respect your own instinct above others, since trusting your own power and knowledge is part of the process of learning to love and honour yourself.

CRYSTAL LOVE-ATTRACTION PROGRAMMING

This ritual follows exactly the same principles as every other ritual you have carried out. The key is to get a picture with feelings attached to it. See yourself on your wedding day, joyfully happy and laughing with friends and family.

Now take that picture in your mind's eye and transfer it into the crystal. Set the crystal on your love altar (see page 131) or another special place. You can also wear the programmed crystal. The crystal will transmit your image to the universe, rather like a beacon flashing out light on a dark night lets people from miles around know where something is. The energies of the programmed crystal beam out to the invisible universe, pulling in the future you have programmed. The more the original image you have programmed in resonates with you, the stronger the force of the crystal.

If your dream partner is taking time to show up, a crystal grid (see opposite) will radiate more power than a single crystal. Place your crystal grid on your love altar or other special place in the home where it won't be interfered with.

OTHER LOVE CRYSTALS

Diamonds Although we associate diamonds with engagement rings and therefore marriage, diamonds aren't as love-attracting as rose quartz. They attract fidelity, long life and sexuality instead.

Emeralds Emeralds are love amplifiers. However, they stimulate love to all things on earth rather than specifically romantic love. If you want to increase your general feelings of love, then wear an emerald ring or pendant. A pendant that rests over the heart chakra (see page 69) will act like a battery, charging the forces of love around you and bringing love into your life from all directions.

Jade This is the stone of the Chinese Goddess of Love and Compassion, Guan Yin (see page 149). It is a healing stone, which also attracts romance and love to you. In addition, this powerful gem attracts prosperity, so if you wear it you will magnetize abundance into your life in many ways.

Black obsidian This gemstone is protective. If you pick up other people's energies too readily and get knocked back by negative atmospheres, then wear this close to your heart so that the energies are deflected from your aura and you receive only the loving energies around you.

Make a crystal love grid

♥ You need eight clear crystals or a mix of crystals and rose quartz. Many crystal shops sell small inexpensive crystals as smooth round stones called 'tumbled stones', which are fine for this purpose. Make sure they are clean.

♥ Select one of the eight crystals to be your 'charging crystal'. Now arrange six of the crystals in a circle with their tips pointing inwards. Place the seventh in the centre. If it has a point, this can point in any direction towards the other stones, but not upwards.

♥ Now set your intention. Ask that your highest spiritual guides, higher self and universal love purify and charge this grid to bring love into your life in a way that is in accordance with your highest good. You can also use this grid to bring in general healing of any issues in your life in accordance with your highest good. If you have any angels who are special to you, ask for their energies as well at this point.

♥ Take your charging crystal in your right hand and imagine channelling this loving, healing energy into each crystal on your grid, flowing the energy through your charging crystal, pointed to each crystal in turn as if the charging crystal is a magic wand.

♥ Finally connect up the grid. Flow the energy through your charging crystal to the centre crystal, then to one of the outer crystals, on to the next crystal and back to the centre so that you make a series of pie segments. Move counter-clockwise around the grid until you close the circle. As you do this, keep your intention clear in your head.

♥ Make sure you always do the ritual with an open mind and heart, bringing in genuinely what is to your higher good and not trying to bring in a particular person, which would be an abuse of this power.

♥ The grid will stay charged for 24 hours. You can recharge it on a daily basis by using the charging crystal and resetting your intention. You can also write your intention on a piece of paper and put it underneath the grid.

IN ESSENCE

What you focus on is what you create in your life. A ritual is a new habit that changes your focus. A ritual may seem to be an everyday or ordinary act, but it is infused with the spiritual energy of the extraordinary. Regular rituals help you to build belief and expectation that your new life will come about because it changes your focus on every level. Absolute focus from your whole self, conscious and unconscious, cannot fail to bring about change in your life. There are many kinds of ritual you can introduce into your life as a way of focusing on love attraction.

Your home is itself a symbol of the self, so anything you do to the home will affect you. By carrying out rituals in your home you intentionally make your home into a living ritual since it is the place that carries the vibration of your thoughts every day.

Give each ritual you do proper attention, time and energy. Begin by being clear each time you carry out a ritual what your intention is for that ritual. The spiritual universe will hear that intention and support you in manifesting it. Carrying out the ritual is the action which lets the universe know that you are putting effort into your part of the co-creation process.

Let your rituals be mirrors to the self by making them activities or objects of beauty. You will be rewarded with the flow of love energy into your life.

MY NOTES

CHAPTER 7

Your spiritual helpers

'IF YOU WANT TO BE LOVED, BE LOVABLE.'

OVID

Within the invisible spiritual universe, there are many spiritual helpers (spirit energies), who are available to you. They can be called on to help you discover your repeating patterns that block love. They can support you during difficult times and they can bring you people and opportunities to create love in your life.

You may or may not have worked with spiritual helpers before. The idea of calling on angels or higher guides for help has become very popular over recent years. You may come from a particular religious tradition where you regularly ask a god or goddess for help. If so, you will be familiar with some of the ideas in this chapter. If not, you may be encountering this technique for the first time. You don't have to have done anything before, or belong to any particular faith or religious practice, to turn to these spiritual helpers. They are always there for you.

In this chapter you will learn:

♥ About three goddesses who will help you with love issues

♥ How to use goddess power to heal and open your heart

♥ How to identify your power animal guide

♥ How to call on angels for help

Calling upon the power of the goddesses

Goddesses are spiritual beings who are there to help us. Whether you are a woman or a man, you can use goddess power to open up your feminine aspect, your attractiveness, your inner and outer beauty and radiance and all aspects of love.

The three goddesses that follow share a similar energy, but each represents a different aspect of this energy. By linking into each of them, you can draw upon their help to heal the parts of you that put a barrier around your heart, and to open up your heart to attract love. You will probably feel that one goddess appeals to you more than the others, even though these are all goddesses through whom you can receive love and healing. Just go with your instinct and draw upon the energy of the one you resonate most with. It will be the energy you most need at this time. Your instinct is always right. Trust it.

For each goddess I have outlined a specific way to draw in their energy through meditation. Generally it is a good idea to practise the meditation at a time you have put aside for this purpose. However, you don't have to limit yourself to this time. After you have become familiar with the energy of the goddess, you can call on her at any time and use her name to calm yourself or to remind yourself to open up your heart immediately. For example, when you are meeting a new person for the first time, simply ask the goddess to be with you. Or perhaps you are out and about and need help to lift your mood, so again call on her by name.

THE GODDESS APHRODITE (VENUS)

Aphrodite (Venus) is the Goddess of Love and Beauty. She is also the goddess of passion and very much associated with sexuality. You can link into her specifically to heal your heart energy and bring new love or passion into your relationships. Her son is Eros (Cupid), who fires the arrows of love and desire into all of us when we meet our romantic partner.

In Greek mythology Aphrodite (Venus) is the daughter of Zeus (Jupiter). The blacksmith god Hephaestus (Vulcan) made her a magic jewelled girdle, which made her irresistible when she wore it. In Ancient Greece the priestesses of Aphrodite represented her energy and it was believed that those who slept with them were worshipping the energy of the goddess. Aphrodite herself was said to have had passionate affairs with many mortals and gods, including Adonis and Ares (Mars).

She has several symbols linked to her energy: the swan, dove, scallop shell, flaming torch, mirror, rose, myrtle and also the pomegranate fruit.

By linking into her energy, either directly or through focusing on one of her symbols through meditation, you can ask for her help.

HOW TO LINK TO APHRODITE (VENUS)

First of all, choose the name you wish to call her – either the Greek Aphrodite or the Latin Venus. They both have slightly different energies, even though the attributes of the goddess in both cultures are basically the same.

Find some space for yourself. Sit quietly and think about how you want to open up your heart to love and passion. Imagine what it will be like when your life is renewed and refreshed and filled with this new feeling.

You might also want to ask for help about a very specific old love pattern you used to have in your life and that you now want to fix. Imagine what it will be like when it has gone forever. What will replace it? What will your life be like?

Get into the mood of the love you want to create. Create yourself a loving and romantic atmosphere. You could light candles or even get dressed in clothes that make you feel romantic or seductive. Play some romantic music in the background. Think about your favourite romantic novel or film – anything that helps to bring the vibration of Aphrodite's (Venus's) love and passion into the moment.

Then imagine she is in front of you and ask for her help to bring this vibration into your life on a daily basis:

'Dear Goddess Venus, I ask that you now open up my heart to receive all the love, beauty and passion that you can bring. I ask that you now release any blocks, illusions and old patterns of love that hold me back from receiving this beautiful love daily so that I radiate love and attract love, filling my whole being so that I resonate with love and light. I ask that you place your rose within my heart as a symbol of this.'

Now see in your mind's eye a rose in your heart chakra (see page 69) with its petals open to symbolize your open heart.

Every morning when you wake up you can remind yourself to open your heart to receive love by visualizing yourself opening up the petals of the rose within your heart.

THE GODDESS GUAN YIN

Guan Yin (pronounced gwan-yin in Chinese, sometimes spelt Kwan Yin or in Japanese Kannon) is the Goddess of Love and Compassion. One of the most popular goddesses in Chinese and East Asian traditions, she is the Eastern equivalent of Aphrodite (Venus) and her name means 'she who hears the cries of the world'.

There are many paintings of Guan Yin and you will find her image all over Asia. She is generally shown rather like a Madonna figure, as a beautiful woman in flowing white robes. In her left hand she holds a white lotus, which signifies purity. There are 32 different forms of Guan Yin. She is often shown as a thousand arms and sometimes a thousand eyes as well, looking in all directions so that she can see and offer mercy to all humanity wherever it is needed.

It is said that Guan Yin was born from a ray of white light that came from the eye of Buddha. Sometimes she carries a vase, which symbolizes compassion and wisdom, a willow branch which symbolizes divine life, or a scroll containing the words of wisdom of Buddha.

HOW TO LINK TO GUAN YIN

Ask Guan Yin to help change your love situation by praying to her image or by using a mantra dedicated to her. 'Mantra' means 'to release the mind'. It calls upon the spiritual energies in the universe to change reality on this earth plane (see page 150). Guan Yin is a healer and it is believed by some that even just saying her name again and again will bring her to you in times of need.

If you want to bring Guan Yin's energy into your home, you could create an altar dedicated to her with a statue or picture of her on it, or add these to an existing altar. Guan Yin loves water, so place a cup of fresh water there daily. Add flowers as a symbol of the feminine energy she represents.

CHANTING MANTRAS

Mantras are chanted as a way of linking into the energy stirred up by the sound of the words. To begin a chant, sit down, straight-backed on a chair or cross-legged. Exhale stale breath from your body at least three times before you begin the chant, to put yourself into the right state and to relax your mind so that you are ready to receive the new energy into your mind, body and spirit. Then begin the chant.

When you chant a mantra regularly you do several things. First of all, on a basic level, chanting is a form of trance or active meditation. It has the benefits of any kind of meditation, which is to make you feel calmer and more at ease. On a spiritual level, chanting links you to pure spiritual consciousness through the energy of the words expressed in the mantra.

By linking in to this energy, you raise your spiritual vibration and expel negative thoughts, opening yourself up to attract blessings and purification.

As you repeat the words again and again the sound and vibration of the mantra enter your consciousness and the energy of your being. As you say the mantra, other thoughts have no room in your mind, so only the thought of the mantra is present.

The more you repeat the mantra, the more it is felt in rhythmic waves in the body and on a soul level. At a certain point of repetition you will feel the change taking place as you reach a point of stillness, even of bliss. After you finish chanting, the effect lasts in your body, just as doing a gym session would have lasting effects on your muscle tone even after you leave the gym.

OM MANI PADME HUM

Om mani padme hum (pronounced ohm-mah-nee-pahd-may-hum), or 'Hail to the jewel of the lotus', is my favourite mantra for calling Guan Yin. It is said that if you chant this mantra a million times you will be transformed as you link permanently to the point of pure consciousness within the universe. Luckily, even chanting the mantra consistently will bring changes into your life.

You can begin chanting softly or loudly, inside your head or saying it out loud, again and again. It may not be possible for you to chant out loud in every instance, but it is better if you can do so at least some of the time. This is because the actual sound of the words causes your throat chakra, the energy centre for communication (see page 69), to feel the vibration of the mantra, and the mantra heals and opens up this centre as you chant. The throat chakra may need opening if you have held back from speaking the truth in past relationships or have in any other way suppressed yourself from speaking up for who you are, which is very common in anybody who has attracted unloving situations in the past.

In Tibet *Om mani padme hum* is often inscribed into stones, which are put into buildings as blessings. You can inscribe the mantra on to a personal stone and either carry it with you or put it on a personal altar.

NAMO GUAN SHI YIN PUSA

Namo guan shi yin pusa (pronounced nah-moh-gwan-shir-yin-poo-sah) means 'I call upon the goddess Guan Yin, who observes the cries of the world.'

This is a second mantra you can use to invoke Guan Yin. In this mantra you call on the goddess directly to request help from her. You can ask for help in times of crisis or again simply to set you on the right path to attract more love into your life.

Chant the mantra a few times and then ask for the help you need.

THE GODDESS GREEN TARA

Green Tara is the Tibetan Buddhist equivalent of the Chinese Guan Yin and was originally an Indian goddess. In Japan she is called Tarani Bosatsu (Bosatsu means Buddha). Tara is the female equivalent of the bodhisattva (an enlightened being) called Avalokitesvara. There are many aspects to Tara, of which Green Tara is one of the most loving. The word 'Tara' means 'star' in Sanskrit, and as your star she can provide you with guidance and navigation as you learn to receive love again. Tara is also known as the liberator or saviour.

She symbolizes grace, beauty and also care and protection. She is a goddess who will be there for you in an emergency as she is also a warrior who helps you to fight fear and overcome obstacles. I would encourage you to link with her energy specifically if you feel that you are facing either internal or external obstacles along your path towards attracting love into your life. Green Tara is a goddess who can really help you to be focused in getting your goals.

She is dressed in silk and jewels and sits on a lotus flower, holding three more in her hand to symbolize the different levels of enlightenment.

OM TARE TUTTARE TURE SOHA

Om tare tuttare ture soha (pronounced om-ta-ray-too-ta-ray-too-ray-so-ha) is Tara's mantra. The mantra asks that the goddess liberates you from suffering and helps you to be balanced in your spirituality.

As you chant, imagine your crown chakra on top of your head opening up to let in the white light of the infinite love within the universe and the abundant love of Green Tara, so that it can flow directly into your heart chakra. Make a decision that this love will fill you up so abundantly that you will always have enough to spare for anybody or anything on the planet that needs love in that particular moment.

This is such a powerful chant that you will feel it reverberate throughout your whole energetic system. Take space each day to meditate on Green Tara if she is the one of the three goddess energies with which you are most in tune.

Remember, when you meditate, wherever possible put yourself in a place free of any distractions, like noise or people walking in on you. The Buddhists call distractions 'meditation thorns', the little day-to-day irritations that take our attention away from the meditation and back to the external world again. Meditation of any form (including chanting) is inner-world work, so keep your space free of mental and physical clutter so that you can turn your attention only to focus on the present moment of connection with the goddess.

Your power animal guide

Working with animal guides is another wonderful, gentle way to open up your heart energy. You have probably heard of shamans who have animal spirits or of witches who use animal familiars to create magic. Many magical and spiritual traditions have used nature spirits for thousands of years as a way to link into particular vibrations. It is almost like taking a shortcut to a particular destination.

Each of us has some animals that we relate to more than others. You may know of people who collect pictures or images of different animals. For some reason I have always been drawn to elephants and the great cats. For years I didn't understand why, until I was taken through a 'totem' meditation to discover the animals whose energies most resonated with my heart and spiritual chakras (see page 69) – lo and behold, these very animals! After doing this I was able to work energetically with these animals for spiritual purposes.

Discovering the animal that resonates with your heart is a lovely way to gently feel loving energy open up in your life and it is a very simple thing to discover.

Once you have identified your heart power animal you can bring it out at any time by intentionally relaxing and following this guided meditation. Spending time in your mind with your heart power animal is a way of opening up to love. Keep pictures or even toys in the form of the animal around your home. You can ask it questions, you can ask it to help you to clear spaces of low energy. It will increasingly help you, the more and more you become connected to it. You can call on the energy of your animal guide to be with you any time you need support or are feeling low.

Meet your power animal guide

♥ Simply sit or lie quietly. Close your eyes and make sure you are comfortable. In your mind's eye open up each of your chakras (see page 69) from the bottom up. See the petals of each chakra opening up to show the beauty of the flower and receive the energy of the universe.

♥ Now take three deep breaths in through your nose and out through your mouth. As you exhale, feel the breath relax every muscle of your body.

♥ Feel your legs and arms relax, your fingers and toes and your neck and head relax.

♥ Imagine that you are walking through a beautiful green meadow into a wood where you can feel the light breeze and smell the scent of the flowers and leaves around you. There are beautiful old and wise trees around you. You are totally connected with nature. You are no different from the flowers or the trees, the sun or the wind.

♥ Stand still amongst the greenery and imagine you can draw up the energy of the earth through your feet into your body. It is a wonderful loving Mother Earth energy. The energy is drawn up through your feet and then up through each of your chakras. Feel the energy coming up through your lower body, filling it up with love. Draw the energy up to the heart.

♥ When you reach the heart you will become aware of your heart chakra, located right in the centre of your chest, opening up. As it opens you become aware of an animal there. You may or may not see it immediately or you may become aware of its name before you see it and feel it. Just let it emerge very gently.

♥ As it emerges I want you to feel the loving energy of your heart power animal. Talk to it. Be with it. Play with it, touch it, stroke it. Love it.

♥ Spend time with your animal and then let it return inside you.

♥ Then let the loving energy in your body expand to fill up every cell of your body. Fill yourself with love and then, when you have done this, simply open your eyes and come back to the room. This is very grounded energy so you should feel peaceful and content.

Help from the angels

An angel is a non-physical being. The name angel means 'messenger of God'. There are many angels who are available to help you and many other guides in the spiritual universe. Like god and goddess spirit energies, angels are available to help you with any area of your life. They also have specializations. The angels who can most help you with love issues are archangels (the highest of the angels) and guardian angels (the angels assigned especially to each of us before we are born). An archangel is a higher form of angel than the guardian angel and so can be called upon when you are in need of extra help.

ARCHANGEL JOPHIEL

All the archangels can help you in many different ways. Archangel Jophiel can help you get out of negative thought patterns, so is a very useful energy when you want to attract love into your life.

Just ask Jophiel for help to make your thoughts more loving, both to yourself and to life in general. Her energy will help this to happen. You can also ask her for help as you start to put your physical home in order. By making your living space more beautiful you are letting her know that you are preparing to welcome in new beauty and love into your life. Call on her help to make your home a magnet for positive and beautiful thought energies every day.

YOUR GUARDIAN ANGEL

Your guardian angel will stay with you your whole life, but other angels are there only if you call, or 'invoke', them and when you focus on forming a link with them. You don't need to give your guardian angel a name. It is fine just to think of your guardian angel as that.

You can ask your guardian angel to make their presence known to you. You may see the angel in a form that is pleasant to you. You may feel the brush of an angel's wings on your shoulder or back to signal that they are there, or feel a tingling on your arm as they connect with you. Your guardian angel may also make their presence known in dreams – look out for helpers appearing in the stories of your dreams.

You can consciously connect with your guardian angel any time just by asking for help. For example, you might say: 'Please help me to achieve this goal' or 'Please help me get the courage I need to sign up to a dating site.'

You can also ask your guardian angel for a sign so that you know that help is coming from the right source. Just say something like: 'Please give me a sign that I am on the right track.'

You may suddenly notice something you haven't noticed before, like an advert that says 'Sign up now!', or you may just get a strong feeling. The more you practise the connection, the better you will become at noticing these subtle angelic messages.

If you are not sure whether messages are coming from your angels, consider whether they serve your ego or the highest good, not only of you, but of other people around you and the world at large. Messages from the angels will always lead to the latter.

CASE STUDY: JULES

Jules had experienced a lot of pain in her childhood because she had seen spiritual guides from a very early age. Her family had thought she was suffering from mental illness and had sent her to a psychiatrist. Later in life she had accepted that she just saw things differently from other people, and didn't tell those who were unlikely to believe her. She left America when she was in her early twenties to try to find a purpose in life. She had an experience in Asia, which set her on the right path.

Jules had been travelling on a bus in Nepal when it almost went off the side, of the road, at the edge of a sharp drop. As she felt the bus tilt to one side with the passengers terrified, she called on her guardian angel for help. Immediately and miraculously the bus tilted back to its centre and the wheels managed to cling to the road. Jules and the other passengers made it to the end of the journey unscathed.

After that experience, Jules began to trust her angels fully. She told me that she called on their help every day to make sure she stayed true to her purpose in life – no matter what other people told her to do – to gain strength and courage in adversity and to bring her love and health. When Jules settled back in the United States she met a delightful man who was very spiritual. They started an organic farm together and, with the help of her angels, Jules now paints and writes creatively. She learned that angels, unlike many people, are unconditional in their love. They won't judge you. You still retain free will so that you can learn from your experience in life, but they will help you when called, 24 hours a day.

IN ESSENCE

The spiritual universe is there to help you in your life. There is always help when you need it. Some of the helpers within the spiritual universe to whom you can turn have specific areas of expertise, including the ability to help with relationships or other love issues.

When you want to connect with a particular spiritual being, the more you find out about them, the more you can tune into their energies.

It is very important that you feel drawn to whichever spiritual helper you work with. Find out as much as possible about the three love goddesses in this chapter. Read about them and do your own research. Decide whose energy you most resonate with by paying attention to how you feel when you think about them. When you have decided which one you want to connect to and ask for help around a particular issues, carry out the devotions to them. You can use the suggestions in this chapter or use your instinct to create your own devotions. In return for your devotion, they will help you.

You can forge a separate relationship with your power animal. This is your personal spiritual animal guide. Its energy will stay by you and be a source of comfort and support.

Ask the angels for help every day to make you stronger, to open your heart and to help you through difficult times.

MY NOTES

CHAPTER 8

Soul mates

'THE MINUTE I HEARD MY FIRST LOVE STORY,
I STARTED LOOKING FOR YOU, NOT KNOWING HOW
BLIND THAT WAS.
LOVERS DON'T FINALLY MEET SOMEWHERE.
THEY'RE IN EACH OTHER ALL ALONG.'
RUMI

People talk a lot about soul mates. They seem to think that there's only one special person for all of us and, when they find this soul mate or 'the one', that will be the end of all difficulties in life.

If they meet a special person and start having difficulties a few months into the relationship, then they become really disillusioned, wondering how this can be the 'right person' for them if there are issues to be resolved.

When you ask the universe to send you a soul mate, the universe will oblige, as it will with all your intentions. However, you may get more than you bargain for. So read on to learn about soul mates, so that you can make the choice as to whether or not this is what you really want.

In this chapter you will learn about:

♥ Soul mates and Karmic ties

♥ Twin souls

♥ Dream journeying

The definition of 'soul mate'

I want to start by clarifying terms and being as precise as possible.

Many people use the term 'soul mate' simply to mean a person who will truly love you and whom you will truly love. From the many experiences I have observed I do believe that anyone can at any time consciously attract a deeply connected, loving relationship to them. If this is what you want to create, then I would leave out the words 'soul mate' when you ask the universe to bring you love and ask instead that the universe brings exactly the right person into your life with whom you can be happy, who will be happy with you and with whom you can give and receive love.

You frame this 'cosmic order' or 'intention' by asking that it happens in exactly the right way for you, so that it is part of a balanced happy life in every other way as well and is 'in accord with the highest good to all concerned'.

A true or Karmic soul mate, however, is not the same thing. If you ask for a true soul mate, you will definitely learn through the experience.

Karmic soul mates

A true soul mate is a very special person. He or she is someone with whom you have a deep spiritual bond. This is a bond which has karma attached to it. This means that when you meet them you will experience a deep sense of connection and bonding, but you won't necessarily stay with them for the rest of your life. You may also experience lots of emotions with them that aren't love.

I believe that many true soul mates have the potential to come into our lives, although it is also possible that you will meet only one in a lifetime. When you meet your Karmic soul mate you both come into each other's lives to teach each other something. You are both here to teach and both here to learn. Through this meeting you are given the opportunity by the universe to understand yourself and your purpose on a deeper level and to grow both spiritually and emotionally.

Meeting a Karmic soul mate and walking your life with them for a short or long time can be the most amazing healing experience you will ever have. They may shift you further along in your life than ever before. Through a true soul mate you can learn to love for the first time, love more deeply or learn any soul lesson that you need. However, I do believe that it is not necessary that a true soul mate is your mate for life. He or she can be. I have seen people meet, part and then come back together after years and stay together forever in total happiness. I have also seen a true soul mate manifested for a short time in a life and then leave after whatever lesson needs to be learned has been learned.

KARMIC TIES

Karmic soul mates come from the same group of souls within the spiritual universe. We reincarnate with them across many lifetimes. Karmic ties are formed between souls in these previous lives. They happen when deep emotions have attached two people together. A Karmic soul mate may have been your lover, but also your brother, your mother or your father.

You may have loved each other. One of you may have loved the other and the other have hated. A Karmic soul mate may have been your enemy as much as your closest friend in a previous lifetime. It is said that any deep emotional bond will link you together across time and space. When the person reappears in this lifetime the karma or lesson from the previous lifetime needs to be resolved. You make this contract with your Karmic soul mate before you are born into this life.

If there has been a Karmic love bond across different lifetimes, when you meet this person they will appear like a whirlwind in your life. Their appearance may disrupt your life and appear to cause problems at first, but if it is a true soul-mate relationship then there is nothing you can do. For example, if you are already in a relationship and a Karmic soul mate appears, then undoubtedly the relationship will be affected. What exactly will happen depends on what the Karmic soul mate has come into your life to teach you on a spiritual level. Your existing relationship may or may not survive. The more important issue will be that you do not resist the lessons, but are ready to hear and observe what you need to know about love – for ultimately the lesson a Karmic soul mate brings is always one about love and healing.

What is important about Karmic soul mates is that you learn and grow and evolve together. Not all the lessons will be comfortable. This is because many of us resist unconditional love in favour of hanging on to what we know. What we resist persists. Love always finds a way through eventually and that is the lesson. Along the way, you will learn forgiveness of self and others, probably slowly, until experience eventually helps you to recognize what you need to understand much more quickly. This is because we always have free will and choice to play the victim for a while, or behave in an unloving way to others.

How will you know whether you are learning from the lesson a Karmic soul mate is bringing? The only measure is love. If you are in pain, you are in lack and not in love. However, if you can move from pain or suffering through forgiveness to love, then you can live a lifetime with a Karmic soul mate in true joy.

CASE STUDY: JASON

Jason was very unhappily married when he met Kate. He fell in love with her immediately. He felt that she was undoubtedly a soul mate because the bond they had was extraordinary. He left his marriage briefly for this woman, but the affair did not last. However, he changed enormously because, for the first time, he realized that he had been closed up emotionally for years, just getting on with work and paying no attention to his family. Although the affair caused a great deal of pain in the short term, in the longer term, when he returned to his family, he began to behave in a very different and much more loving way to everyone and has now been happily married for 20 years and is much more involved in daily family life, having deliberately retired from his over-demanding job.

Twin souls

The term 'twin souls', or 'twin rays', is another description that you may come across. Many people believe that a twin soul is the other half of your soul, which has been divided into two. The soul experiences life on the earth as male and female (yang and yin), so your twin soul appears in the opposite gender to you.

When you meet your twin soul, this is what many people mean as the 'one'. You have the feeling of being totally whole for the first time in your life. There will be a strong psychic bond between the two of you. You may really feel that you understand what the other person feels or is about to say. You will feel a deep love and trust.

Again there are as many theories about twin souls as there are about soul mates. It is possible that we do not get the chance to meet a twin soul until we have learned the lessons of many true soul-mate encounters because we won't be ready. A twin soul can only come into your life if you have grown sufficiently on a spiritual level to be ready for this intense relationship. A twin-soul relationship is based only on love, so won't come if you generally operate out of neediness, ego or anger.

CASE STUDY: JAKE

Many people finally meet their twin soul after they have experienced a time of profound spiritual change. It is often a meeting that comes about through extraordinary synchronicity. Here's an example of this sort of coincidence.

Jake lived in South Africa for nearly 30 years. After he moved to New York, he experienced a real 'dark night of the soul'. He went through a number of losses and bereavements before he came out the other side of this period a very much humbler and more spiritual person.

He joined a dating site and met Prudence, a lovely South African girl. They discovered the most extraordinary number of synchronicities in their backgrounds. They had been to the same school in South Africa. They had lived a street away from one another. Then they had both moved to New York in the same year. They had also both been married. Prudence had divorced a month earlier, Jake a year earlier. At the time Prudence divorced, Jake had just made the decision to start dating and a few weeks later he found the dating site online where he met Prudence.

The reason, from a spiritual point of view, that these two souls couldn't unite earlier was that both of them had to find a spiritual purpose by themselves first. They had to find resilience in their soul and heal what needed to be healed before they could unite, so that their egos didn't drive each other away.

DIVINE PURPOSE

It is said that when you meet your twin soul, it is not just to experience love on this earth, but to fulfil a divine purpose. When twin souls come together their experience on this earth is magnified. They are able to achieve more than each could separately, not necessarily in terms of material success, but with a purpose that brings more love to the world.

When you meet your twin soul, you will be filled with unconditional love. Sometimes people become obsessed with another person. They need to be with them 24 hours a day and to know what they are doing and feeling and thinking. They assume this is because this is the 'one' who is meant for them. However, this is not a twin-soul situation. Life with a twin soul is never co-dependent. You aren't needy of each other. It is certainly intense because you have met the 'other half' of you. However, it is always unconditional and you find that you are able to be utterly honest with each other because you don't wish to judge each other in any way. Indeed, any neediness you may have experienced in past relationships will be replaced by a common desire to grow together emotionally and spiritually. Your souls know that you have a bond that will outlast life on this earth.

Not all of us will meet a twin soul in our lifetimes, nor would we wish to as we are not all spiritually ready. Most of us will meet Karmic soul mates and go through many experiences and lessons. As we do this we grow and experience more and more love in our lives each time. We become stronger in our sense of self, and happier. There are always ups and downs in life, but the more we learn how to let go of problems and receive love, the more our lives will be filled with love. Don't worry about making mistakes in your relationships or picking the wrong person. As long as you become open to unconditional love it will find you because it is within you.

Dream journeying

If you yearn for a true soul mate or twin-soul experience, you can bring it into your life through dream journeying.

Your soul is free to travel at night and meet other souls. Once you establish contact with another soul in your dream world, you can ask him or her to come to you in the physical world. You have only to desire it to happen and it will.

Remember, though, there is always a time lag, as the story of Carlos in the case study overleaf shows.

When I was first told Carlos's story what struck me most was that they hadn't both recognized each other immediately. I do think from my own experiences and from those of my clients that this is very common. We are often given more than one opportunity to meet our true soul mate. If we don't take it and it is an important connection, then luckily the same person will come back.

I would also say that it is important always to be open when somebody comes into your life. Significant love connections don't announce themselves with a big flag on them saying: 'Hey, I am your soul mate' or 'Hey, I am your twin soul.' First appearances can be very deceptive. A bond that is so clear on the dream plane has to get past all your unconscious prejudices and defences on the earth plane. Your true soul mate may be very slim while you have always been physically attracted to people who are a little cuddlier. If that's the case, then make sure you look past the superficial or you might miss out on someone who can love you forever (perhaps in more than one lifetime).

If you do keep an open mind then eventually the love bond on the dream plane will draw you together and you will recognize each other. Clearly, though, it is much easier if you don't put up lots of barriers to begin with.

CASE STUDY: CARLOS

A writer, Carlos, who is very knowledgeable about spiritual matters, met his twin soul in this way. Carlos deliberately asked to meet his twin soul in his dreams.

He remembered dream after dream where he spent time with a beautiful woman. He told me that each morning when he woke up after one of these dreams he felt the love from having been with her in the spiritual universe. Each dream would follow the same pattern. He would walk through a wood along a path where the wood opened out on to a meadow. He would ask to see his twin soul and a woman would appear. She would reach out her hand to him, but he could never see her face. In the dream they would talk about being together and the lives they had shared before. Carlos longed to meet her, but had no idea how she would come to him and couldn't get any message from his dream that would help.

At the time he was dreaming of his twin soul he lived in California. He dream journeyed for at least six months but never re-created that feeling with any woman he met in his work or personal life. Then one day he received a letter from Natalia, a woman he didn't know who lived in

Europe. She had read about the work he did and invited him to come to lecture in Europe. She was willing to pay all his fares and accommodation for the trip, so he had very little to lose.

When Carlos arrived in Europe, Natalia looked very surprised to see him. After a day, she confessed the reason why. She told him that she too had been dream journeying. She was convinced that Carlos was the man she had been meeting in her dreams and that they were destined to be together and marry.

At first, Carlos was very reluctant to believe Natalia. She came from a very different, much richer background from him and he wasn't at all certain that they had such a strong connection. Natalia bravely kept insisting she was right even though, as she later recalled, she would normally have been embarrassed to have put herself forward in this way.

Carlos was in Europe for about a week. He gave his talks and was due to leave two days later. Then he had a dream. In the dream he walked along the path to his meadow once more. His twin soul appeared. She reached out her hand and, for the first time, he saw her face. Yes, as I am sure you guessed, it was Natalia.

Carlos told me that as soon as he admitted that connection to Natalia, they started to find their bond on the material plane as well. They began to feel closer and closer, driven by a feeling of familiarity and gradually by love. They also realized how much of a spiritual purpose they shared and realized that this was probably why they had been drawn together as true soul mates in this lifetime. Happily, they overcame many hurdles, including family opposition, and they are now married and live and work together, helping many people to improve their lives.

LIKE ATTRACTS LIKE

By the way, you have no doubt heard people say 'opposites attract'. Well, a soul mate doesn't work like that. It works on a 'like attracts like basis.' When you meet a Karmic soul mate or your twin soul, then it is going to be because you are alike on a deep soul level. You may, like Carlos and Natalia, speak different languages, live in different countries, come from different cultural and wealth backgrounds or have very different jobs, but on a soul level there will be a basic likeness that binds you together. The more you get to know each other through love, the more you will discover that mirror within each of you.

YOUR DREAM JOURNEY TO MEET YOUR KARMIC SOUL MATE

Remember, when you desire something, focus on it with all your attention and it will come to you. This is the Law of Attraction. Ask each night before you go to sleep that you meet the right person to be with you in this lifetime and at this point in your life. Ask that you see him or her and talk to him or her. I use this language very precisely so that whoever manifests brings you the life experiences you need at this time.

If you can lucid dream, as I hope you will find easy with practice, then tell your Karmic soul mate where you live and ask that he/she comes to you. Then hand the manner in which this happens over to the spiritual universe, trusting that it knows much better than us what soul experiences we need at this time on earth. You can, however, ask that this be speeded up 'under divine law' and that the universe removes any obstacles to that happening immediately.

You can also ask that your true soul mate gives you some message or means of identifying himself or herself on the earth plane (although this doesn't always happen, as part of your lesson may be to learn to recognize your true soul mate).

Get used to doing this regularly so that when you meet this true soul mate you are very familiar with their energies. This will make you much more able to identify them when you do meet on the earth plane.

Personally, I like to add one more request, although this comes with a health warning as well. I ask that any lessons I need to learn that are preventing me from meeting my true soul mate at once are given to me immediately – in other words, 'bring it on'. These lessons are going to bring me experiences that aren't always comfortable (that's why they are lessons), but are necessary for my spiritual growth, so personally I would rather get them all out of the way in this lifetime. You can choose to do the same or not. It depends how much spiritual growth you are up for this time around! (I always was a bit of a swot at school and now I have become an ambitious spiritual one, too!)

Recognizing your Karmic soul mate/ twin soul

Recognition is not necessarily instant as you will see from the examples that are described in this chapter.

The only way to recognize your mate is to *feel*, not *think*. At a certain point in your relationship you will have a feeling that begins with familiarity and trust and then opens up to love. This familiarity comes from the fact that you have met before, on the dream plane and in other lifetimes.

If you are forced apart for any reason, then you feel the loss very clearly in your heart chakra (see page 69). (This is very different from the loss of someone you are obsessed with or needy of, but don't actually love – when the loss is felt in the solar plexus chakra.)

THE HEAVEN-SENT MARRIAGE

When you finally meet on the earth plane your Karmic soul mate/twin soul you have met in your dreams, you have the opportunity because of the deep bond to overcome past Karmic lessons and bring about a blissful union, which is sometimes referred to as the 'heaven-sent marriage'.

This will not happen straight away. There are two ways we can come together with another person: on a soul level or a personality level. The desires of the personality can get in the way of love and a soul bond. The personality may want that tall, dark handsome man. The soul wants the short, blond man. If the personality digs its heels in, then the soul has to wait until the personality issues are resolved.

Your heaven-sent marriage is going to take work and commitment. That's why not all true soul-mate unions are forever. If you still have thoughts and beliefs that reject love, you are going to need to keep healing them, otherwise your true soul mate will mirror them back to you.

If you feel anger, then that's your personality playing up. Take note of what's going on and the thoughts that are coming up. Are they lack thoughts or abundant thoughts (see page 21)?

If you feel depressed, then you are putting out too much energy and thinking about what other people think of you. If you feel rejected, then you are rejecting yourself. These are all personality issues and do not come from the soul. It is your wrong thinking and illusions that bring pain, not your true soul mate.

When you feel that there is someone for you in times of emotional or spiritual hardship, then that is caused by the souls of you and your mate touching each other and supporting each other. Life with a true soul mate won't always be bliss, but it will always be held together by this deep feeling of love.

When you meet your right mate and see beyond the day-to-day trivial disputes brought about by the personality, it's as if you both now have a foundation under your lives. You can never fall through that foundation. Whatever happens, your love operates as a support there to catch you. You come together, grow together, find passion together and purpose together.

IN ESSENCE

The future you want comes about partly through your own creation and partly through the creation of the universe. At times the universe gives you opportunities to learn as a way of developing as a spiritual being. One of these ways is to bring people into your life who can teach you something you haven't had the opportunity to learn before or have not been willing to learn. We talk about soul mates, but this is a much misused and misunderstood word. Do you really want a true karmic soul mate in your life? Have you met a twin soul? Have you met someone you think might be a karmic soul mate?

If you think that you have or want this experience, be open and willing to learn from what happens. Recognize that your experience isn't necessarily going to be easy, but it will be to your higher good. Ask the universe what this person brings to you in terms of learning for your spiritual development. Remember they may or may not stay in your life, but the knowledge you gain from the experience will stay with you whatever happens.

MY NOTES

CHAPTER 9

Get ready for love

'THERE ARE TWO WAYS TO LIVE YOUR LIFE.
ONE IS AS THOUGH NOTHING IS A MIRACLE.
THE OTHER IS AS THOUGH EVERYTHING
IS A MIRACLE.'

ALBERT EINSTEIN

Okay, so what now? You may have already found that things have changed. Or maybe the change hasn't quite happened yet. Or perhaps a lot of change has happened. What do you do next?

Change is a journey. It may happen in small incremental steps or it may happen all in one day when you least expect it. I don't know which way it will happen for you because we are all different. All I can tell you is that, if you make a change within yourself, it is impossible that there will not be some change as a consequence in your life. Internal change equals external change. As soon as you take action towards a new future, the new future is on its way.

In this chapter you will learn about:

♥ Trusting the universe

♥ The love-attraction checklist

♥ Happy endings

When will my new future happen?

'When?' is the question I am most frequently asked. How long do I need to wait? This depends partly on your belief system and any timing you have set for your vision to manifest, and partly on the rules we all operate under as human beings. You are of course a human being and a human being, in the world of matter operates according to the rules of time and space.

Of course, if you really think about it, thank goodness that we do have time and space in this universe. If I ask for a new home, kitchen, lover, job, or whatever, do I really want them all tumbling down my chimney in one go? Would I be ready to have my future all in one go? From my experience, change happens at exactly the time I am ready for it, even though I often long to speed things up.

Nevertheless, I am certain I am not alone in having found this enormously frustrating at times. Everyone I know who consciously does any kind of manifestation technique gets frustrated waiting. But sometimes time and space help us. Things happen at particular times because the universe really does appear to know when the time is right. We may really want something to happen immediately, but that doesn't mean that it is necessarily the best thing for us. Actually the universe has tested me several times over the years. I have met someone twice in the past and not noticed them, then years later met them when I was ready to be with them. I was offered wealth at a time it meant nothing to me and rejected it, then when I wanted it again, I appreciated it much more for the time I had spent without it. Why did it happen when it did? Well, my beliefs really needed to change and as soon as I had put the effort into changing them and getting really clear about what I wanted, and why that was really right for me, the universe responded immediately.

I know, I know. You're still thinking, 'But I am ready now!'

All I can say is please really *trust*. Trust that a transformation in your life is under way now. Trust that the universe knows the right timing for you. You are already stepping into a new reality – a reality you have asked for. Be patient. Trying to push things to happen or being over-attached to your outcome won't bring it nearer faster. A gentle focus on what you want to bring into your life is quite enough.

BE PATIENT

Now, align yourself to your future with gratitude to allow the flow of love and abundance into your life. Believe that it has already fully manifested in your life.

Trust is enough. Once you have planted the seeds of your thoughts in the universe, the universe knows what you want and is already changing the circumstances of your life. It's just like when you plant a seed in your garden, there are all sorts of things you can't see happening under the ground, but when the earth is ready to receive the flower, up it comes.

Carry on with your life, finding new enthusiasms and new times for fun and joy. Carry on noticing all the blessings you already have in your life. Step by step, piece by piece, you are creating the life you have always wanted, bringing towards you more and more of the experiences you always dreamed of having and changing into the person you always intended to be. Be patient and allow the universe to open up your miraculous new beginning for you.

When in doubt...

But what if you doubt? What if it is taking too long? What if you think it will happen, but you don't absolutely know that it will happen? Or you think that you may know, but you aren't certain if you know you know ... and so on?

Yes, it's hard to read and make sense of those sentences. It is even more muddling when they are thoughts going round and round in your brain. If you start doubting or being not sure, or getting confused, or over-analyzing or getting in any other way stuck about what you think you can manifest in your life, I want you to just stop. Take a big deep breath and go back to basics.

Opposite is a final checklist to enable you to make sure that you attract the most wonderful life.

THE LOVE-ATTRACTION CHECKLIST

♥ Check where, and if, you are really stuck. Reread the chapters that can be most helpful to you. Check out the Love-attraction Formula (see page 9). Notice if there is anything you have forgotten to do or whether there are any steps you have missed or rushed through.

♥ Check your beliefs. Do you believe it is OK to attract love? Do you believe that you *deserve* to attract love? Do you believe you *can* attract love? Have you let go of lack and woken up to a new way of thinking that you can attract an abundance of love into your life as much as anyone else?

♥ Check that you have healed what you needed to have healed. Have you truly forgiven who and what needs to be forgiven in your life, *including* yourself? Have you noticed the good things you have learned from the past as well as the things you no longer wish to keep?

♥ Check your intention. Do you have a clear vision of what you are going to bring into your life? Do you have pictures – either on your love treasure map (see page 81) or in your mind's eye, or both – of the sort of life you will be living when it is filled with love? Are you certain that you believe this is possible and probable, so that it has moved from a 'want' to a 'when'?

♥ Check your own self-love. What do you really feel about yourself? Be totally truthful. I don't just mean when you are feeling at your best, but *every day*, no matter who is present or not present in your life.

♥ Check your daily habits. Have you built into your life regular rituals that help you to maintain the belief that you are going to attract this love into your life? Have you identified your power animal of the heart? Have you decided which form of the love goddess you are most in tune with? If so, have you asked for help? Make it a habit. Build your connection with the spiritual universe and the energies will come closer to you and help you every day in your life.

♥ Check your dreams. What is going on in them? Are they indicating how near you are to attracting your new life? Are they indicating any blocks to be resolved or any thought patterns still present that need a bit of change? If so, make the change. Have you tried waking dreaming? If 'no', give it a go. If 'yes', how regularly? Take a week and use waking dreaming to build your dreams. Flow your feelings into them and let them become a magnet for love.

Happy endings

Finally I want to take you back to Lucy, whom I told you about in Chapter 1 (see page 14). Change happened to Lucy when she first started using the Law of Attraction. She rang me up out of the blue about a year after she had started making changes in her thinking.

A year previously, we had sat in a café and Lucy had described the life she wanted with a wonderful man who would love her for who she was. We talked through what she wanted for over an hour, but I could tell she wasn't totally certain that she could really create this change in her life. However, something was set in motion because a few months later she started to make changes one after another.

First, Lucy made the decision to move to a different house as she had stayed in the house where she had lived with her husband. She had thrown out all her old clutter, then she started buying new clothes and new furniture. There were very few men in her life at this time. She was surrounded by single women who were constantly complaining about the terrible time they had gone through with men. As soon as she moved house, which was a huge decision for her, she got offered the chance of a new career as well. She started going out and meeting lots of new people and getting her confidence back. She didn't meet a boyfriend immediately, but was already much happier.

Then one day Lucy gave me a call. 'The strangest thing has happened,' she said. 'I had just stopped looking for a man and I had decided to get on with my life. Actually I just thought life is too short to worry any more and I decided to be happy with what I had. It was almost a year to the day when I made that decision that I got an email. I was going to delete it because I didn't recognize the address and thought it might be spam. Something made me open it.'

The email was from a former boyfriend of Lucy's from many years ago –
Bob, the last boyfriend she had had before she had met and married Steven.
They had been together for a year or so, but then Bob had moved abroad to do
voluntary work and, this being before everybody had email and used Facebook,
they had lost touch. It turned out that Bob had been trying to track down Lucy
for a whole year – again, amazingly around the time Lucy had sat in the café
with me talking about the kind of life she wanted. He had sent a card to her old
family address, he had emailed old friends, but no one was in touch with her.
Bob was about to give up when he managed to track down an old girlfriend
of Lucy's. Although she hadn't been in touch with Lucy for a while herself,
she did give him Lucy's email.

There is a real fairy-tale happy ending here. Lucy was very nervous about
meeting Bob again after so many years, but when she did, it felt so natural to
both of them being together that they moved in together after only three months.

'I just knew it was safe to be with him because he loved me before,' Lucy told
me, 'but also because I had been through all those big changes by myself over the
last year. I felt braver about life and I knew that it was safe to be myself with
someone again.'

IN ESSENCE

Now that you have reached the end of this book my wish for you is that your story has a happy ending as well.

Take all the time you need to change your life and make it how you want to be.

Learn through practice how the Law of Attraction can bring love into your life every day.

Change the story of your past to a happy one. Recognize the perfect, loving being you are. Start now with a fresh sheet of paper and begin to dream the life you want to create.

Look to the spiritual universe and the helpers who live within it to help you realize your dream of a loving future.

Rely on the Law of Attraction as a perfect means of bringing the future you want into your life.

Set your intention to co-create your future and show your commitment to the universe by taking action towards what you want every day.